Classic Dinners

Everyday Cookbook

STAR FIRE

This is a Star Fire book
First published in 2006

06 08 10 09 07

1 3 5 7 9 10 8 6 4 2

Star Fire is part of
The Foundry Creative Media Company Limited
Crabtree Hall, Crabtree Lane, Fulham, London, SW6 6TY

Visit our website: www.star-fire.co.uk

ISBN-10: 1-84451-532-X ISBN-13: 978-1-84451-532-5
Special Edition: ISBN-10: 1-84451-575-3 ISBN-13: 978-1-84451-575-2

The CIP record for this book is available from the British Library.

Printed in China

ACKNOWLEDGEMENTS

Publisher and Creative Director: Nick Wells
Editorial Planning: Rosanna Singler
Design and Production: Chris Herbert, Mike Spender, Colin Rudderham and Claire Walker

Authors: Catherine Atkinson, Juliet Barker, Gina Steer, Vicki Smallwood,
Carol Tennant, Mari Mererid Williams, Elizabeth Wolf-Cohen and Simone Wright
Editorial: Sara Goulding and Sara Robson
Photography: Colin Bowling, Paul Forrester and Stephen Brayne
Home Economists and Stylists: Jacqueline Bellefontaine,
Mandy Phipps, Vicki Smallwood and Penny Stephens

All props supplied by Barbara Stewart at Surfaces

NOTE
Recipes using uncooked eggs should be avoided by infants,
the elderly, pregnant women and anyone suffering from an illness.

Contents

Soups & Starters

Main Meals

Vegetables & Salads

Desserts

Hygiene in the Kitchen

It is important to remember that many foods can carry some form of bacteria. In most cases, the worst it will lead to is a bout of food poisoning or gastroenteritis, although for certain people this can be serious. The risk can be reduced or eliminated, however, by good hygiene and proper cooking.

Do not buy food that is past its sell-by date and do not consume food that is past its use-by date. When buying food, use the eyes and nose. If the food looks tired, limp or a bad colour or it has a rank, acrid or simply bad smell, do not buy or eat it under any circumstances.

Take special care when preparing raw meat and fish. A separate chopping board should be used for each, and the knife, board and your hands should be thoroughly washed before handling or preparing any other food.

Regularly clean, defrost and clear out the refrigerator or freezer – it is worth checking the packaging to see exactly how long each product is safe to freeze. Avoid handling food if suffering from an upset stomach as bacteria can be passed on through food preparation.

Dish cloths and tea towels must be washed and changed regularly. Ideally use disposable cloths which should be replaced on a daily basis. More durable cloths should be left to soak in bleach, then washed in the washing machine at a high temperature.

Keep your hands, cooking utensils and food preparation surfaces clean and do not allow pets to climb on to any work surfaces.

Buying

Avoid bulk buying where possible, especially fresh produce such as meat, poultry, fish, fruit and vegetables. Fresh foods lose their nutritional value rapidly, so buying a little at a time minimises loss of nutrients. It also means your fridge will not be so full, which reduces the effectiveness of the refrigeration process.

When buying prepackaged goods such as cans or pots of cream and yogurts, check that the packaging is intact and not damaged or pierced at

all. Cans should not be dented, pierced or rusty. Check the sell-by dates even for cans and packets of dry ingredients such as flour and rice. Store fresh foods in the refrigerator as soon as possible – not in the car or the office.

When buying frozen foods, ensure that they are not heavily iced on the outside and that the contents feel completely frozen. Ensure that the frozen foods have been stored in the cabinet at the correct storage level and the temperature is below -18°C/-0.4°F. Pack in cool bags to transport home and place in the freezer as soon as possible after purchase.

Preparation

Make sure that all work surfaces and utensils are clean and dry. Hygiene should be given priority at all times. Separate chopping boards should be used for raw and cooked

meats, fish and vegetables. Currently, a variety of good quality plastic boards come in various designs and colours. This makes differentiating easier and the plastic has the added hygienic advantage of being washable at high temperatures in the dishwasher. If using the board for fish, first wash in cold water, then in hot to prevent odour. Also remember that knives and utensils should always be thoroughly cleaned after use.

When cooking, be particularly careful to keep cooked and raw food separate to avoid any contamination. It is worth washing all fruits and vegetables regardless of whether they are going to be eaten raw or lightly cooked. This rule should apply even to prewashed herbs and salads.

Do not reheat food more than once. If using a microwave, always check that the food is piping hot all the way through – in theory, the food should reach 70°C/158°F and needs to be cooked at that temperature for at least three minutes to ensure that all bacteria are killed.

All poultry must be thoroughly thawed before using, including chicken and poussin. Remove the food to be thawed from the freezer and place in a shallow dish to contain the juices. Leave the food in the refrigerator until it is completely thawed. A 1.4 kg/3 lb whole chicken will take about 26–30 hours to thaw. To speed up the process, immerse the chicken in cold water, making sure that the water is changed regularly. When the joints can move freely and no ice crystals remain in the cavity, the bird is completely thawed.

Once thawed, remove the wrapper and pat the chicken dry. Place the chicken in a shallow dish, cover lightly and store as close to the base of the refrigerator as possible. The chicken should be cooked as soon as possible. Some foods can be cooked from frozen including many prepacked foods such as soups, sauces, casseroles and breads. Where applicable follow the manufacturers' instructions.

Vegetables and fruits can also be cooked from frozen, but meats and fish should be thawed first. The only time food can be refrozen is when the food has been thoroughly thawed then cooked. Once the food has cooled then it can be frozen again, but it should only be stored for one month.

All poultry and game (except for duck) must be cooked thoroughly. When cooked, the juices will run clear on the thickest part of the bird – the best area to try is usually the thigh. Other meats, like minced meat and pork should be cooked right the way through. Fish should turn opaque, be firm in texture and break easily into large flakes.

When cooking leftovers, make sure they are reheated until piping hot and that any sauce or soup reaches boiling point first.

Storing, Refrigerating and Freezing

Meat, poultry, fish, seafood and dairy products should all be refrigerated. The temperature of the refrigerator should be between 1–5°C/34–41°F while the freezer temperature should not rise above -18°C/-0.4°F.

To ensure the optimum refrigerator and freezer temperature, avoid leaving the door open for long periods of time. Try not to overstock the refrigerator as this reduces the airflow inside and therefore the effectiveness in cooling the food within.

When refrigerating cooked food, allow it to cool down quickly and completely before refrigerating. Hot food will raise the temperature of the refrigerator and possibly affect or spoil other food stored in it.

Food within the refrigerator and freezer should always be covered. Raw and cooked food should be stored in separate parts of the refrigerator. Cooked food should be kept on the top shelves of the refrigerator, while raw meat, poultry and fish should be placed on bottom shelves to avoid

drips and cross-contamination. It is recommended that eggs should be refrigerated in order to maintain their freshness and shelf life.

Take care that frozen foods are not stored in the freezer for too long. Blanched vegetables can be stored for one month; beef, lamb, poultry and pork for six months and unblanched vegetables and fruits in syrup for a year. Oily fish and sausages should be stored for three months. Dairy products can last four to six months, while cakes and pastries can be kept in the freezer for three to six months.

High Risk Foods

Certain foods may carry risks to people who are considered vulnerable such as the elderly, the ill, pregnant women, babies, young infants and those suffering from a recurring illness.

It is advisable to avoid those foods listed below which belong to a higher-risk category.

There is a slight chance that some eggs carry the bacteria salmonella. Cook the eggs until both the yolk and the white are firm to eliminate this risk. Pay particular attention to dishes and products incorporating lightly cooked or raw eggs which should be eliminated from the diet. Hollandaise sauce, mayonnaise, mousses, soufflés and meringues all use raw or lightly cooked eggs, as do custard-based dishes, ice creams and sorbets. These are all considered high-risk foods to the vulnerable groups mentioned above.

Certain meats and poultry also carry the potential risk of salmonella and so should be cooked thoroughly

until the juices run clear and there is no pinkness left. Unpasteurised products such as milk, cheese (especially soft cheese), pâté, meat (both raw and cooked) all have the potential risk of listeria and should be avoided.

When buying seafood, buy from a reputable source which has a high turnover to ensure freshness. Fish should have bright clear eyes, shiny skin and bright pink or red gills. The fish should feel stiff to the touch, with a slight smell of sea air and iodine. The flesh of fish steaks and fillets should be translucent with no signs of discolouration. Molluscs such as scallops, clams and mussels are sold fresh and are still alive. Avoid any that are open or do not close when tapped lightly. In the same way, univalves such as cockles or winkles should withdraw back into their shells when lightly prodded. When choosing cephalopods such as squid and octopus they should have a firm flesh and pleasant sea smell.

As with all fish, whether it is shellfish or seafish, care is required when freezing it. It is imperative to check whether the fish has been frozen before. If it has been frozen, then it should not be frozen again under any circumstances.

Pasta Techniques and Tips

Steps to Cooking Perfect Pasta

Follow a few simple rules to ensure that your pasta is cooked to perfection every time:

1 Choose a big saucepan – there needs to be plenty of room for the pasta to move around during cooking so that it does not stick together. The most convenient type of saucepan has a built-in perforated inner pan, so that the pasta can be lifted out of the water and drained as soon as it is cooked.

2 Cook the pasta in a large quantity of fast-boiling, well-salted water; ideally about 4 litres/7 pints of water and 1½–2 tablespoons of salt for every 350 g/12 oz–450 g/1 lb of pasta. Some cooks say that the addition of 1–2 teaspoons of olive or sunflower oil not only helps to stop the water boiling over but also helps to prevent the pasta from sticking. However, other cooks believe that as long as the saucepan is large enough and the water is on a full-rolling boil, the pasta will not stick together nor will the water boil over.

3 Tip in the pasta all at once, give it a stir and cover with a lid. Quickly bring back to a rolling boil then remove the lid – do not cover with a lid during cooking. Once it is boiling, turn down the heat to medium-high and cook the pasta for the required time. It should be 'al dente' which literally translates as 'to the tooth' and means that the pasta should be tender, but still firm to the bite. Test frequently towards the end of cooking time; the only way to do this is to take out a piece and try it. Stir the pasta occasionally during cooking with a wooden spoon or fork to make sure that it does not stick to the pan.

4 As soon as the pasta is ready, drain in a colander (or by lifting the draining pan up and out of the water if you have a pasta pot with an inner drainer). Give it a shake, so that any trapped water can drain out. At this stage you can toss the pasta in a little oil or butter if you are not mixing it with a sauce. Reserve a little of the cooking water to stir into the pasta, this not only helps to thin the sauce if necessary, but also helps prevent the cooked pasta sticking together as it cools.

Some pastas need a little more care when cooking than others. Never stir stuffed pastas vigorously, or they may split open and the filling will be lost in the cooking water. When cooking long, dried pasta such as spaghetti, you will need to coil the pasta into the water as it starts to soften. Hold one end of the strands of spaghetti and push the other to the bottom of the pan, coiling them round, and using a wooden spoon or fork, when the boiling water gets too close to your hand.

An alternative cooking method is to add the pasta to boiling salted water as before, then boil rapidly for 2 minutes. Cover the pan with a tight-fitting lid and turn off the heat. Leave to stand for the full cooking time, then drain and serve in the usual way. Pasta may also be cooked successfully in a microwave, although it does not cook any faster than on the hob. Put the pasta in a large bowl, add salt, then pour over enough boiling water to cover the pasta by at least 2.5 cm/1 inch. Microwave on high (100% power) for the times given below. Allow the pasta to stand for 2–3 minutes before draining.

Pasta Cooking Times

Start timing from the moment that the pasta returns to the boil; not from when it was added. Use a kitchen timer if possible, as even a few seconds too long may spoil the pasta.

Fresh 2–3 minutes for thin noodles (although very fine pastas may be ready within seconds of the pasta boiling), thick noodles and shapes 3–4 minutes and filled pastas 5–7 minutes.

Dried 8–12 minutes; filled pastas can take up to 20 minutes to cook, however, you should always check the packet instructions, as some pastas labelled 'quick cook' only take about 4 minutes.

Serving Quantities

As an approximate guide, allow 75–125 g (3–4 oz) uncooked pasta per person. Obviously the amount will depend on whether the pasta is being served for a light or main meal and the type of sauce that it is being served with.

Matching Pasta Types and Sauces

It is entirely up to you which pasta you serve with which sauce but in general, heavier sauces with large chunks of meat or vegetables go less with pastas that will trap the sauce and meat in curls and hollows, such as penne, shells, riagatoni or spirals. On the other hand, soft fluid sauces suit long pastas such as linguine, pappardelle, or tagliatelle.

Classic Sauces

Alla Carbonara Pasta with ham, eggs and cream – the heat of the pasta cooks the eggs to thicken the sauce.

Alla Napoletana Made from fresh tomatoes, but with olive oil, garlic and onions.

All'arrabiata A hot sauce with red chillies, tomatoes and chopped bacon.

All'aglio e Olio Pasta with olive oil and finely chopped garlic.

Alla Marinara A fresh tomato and basil sauce, sometimes with wine (not seafood).

Con Ragu Meat sauce from Bologna (known as bolognaise sauce in English), often made with half minced pork and half minced beef. This is traditionally served with tagliatelle and not spaghetti.

Serving Pasta

In Italy, pasta is usually dressed with the sauce before serving to combine the flavours, but you can top the pasta with the sauce if you prefer, in which case, toss it in a little olive oil or butter to give it an attractive sheen. Cook the sauce and pasta so that they will both be ready at the same time; most sauces can be left to stand for a few minutes and reheated when the pasta is ready. If the pasta is ready before the sauce, drain it, and return to the pan with a tight-fitting lid – it should be fine for a few minutes. Always serve in warmed serving bowls or plates, as pasta loses heat very quickly.

Serving Wines with Pasta

If possible, choose a wine that comes from the same region as the dish you are serving. If there is wine in the sauce, you will be able to serve the rest of the bottle with your meal, so make sure you choose one that you enjoy drinking. Otherwise, pick a wine that matches the strongest-flavoured ingredient in the sauce. Rich, meaty sauces or highly spiced ones with lots of garlic need a robust, full-bodied wine to go with them. Of course, there is no reason why you should stick to Italian wines and if you are serving an oriental pasta dish you may opt for lager or other drinks. Below are ten well-known types of Italian wine.

White Wines
Chardonnay This wine is produced in many parts of the world and is wonderful served with fish dishes. The Italian chardonnay has a faint lemony flavour.

Frascati This wine is made near Rome and is one of the most popular Italian wines. It is crisp and fruity and has quite a lot of body. It goes well with most foods.

Orvieto This wine is named after the town of the same name, just north of Rome. It is dry and soft with a slightly nutty and fruity flavour and is good for summer drinking and serving with fish and white meats.

Soave This wine is one of Italy's most famous wines. The best ones have a distinct hint of almonds and are dry and crisp. It goes well with shellfish, chicken and light vegetable pasta sauces.

Verdiccho This wine comes in a carved amphora bottle and in Italy is known as La Lollobrigida. A crisp, clean and dry white wine with a slightly metallic edge, it is best when served with fish and seafood.

Red Wines
Barbaresco This wine is full-bodied with an intense flavour and a high tannin content. It teams well with rich pasta dishes, especially beef.

Bardolino This is light and fruity with an almost cherry and slightly bitter almond taste; perfect for duck and game.

Barolo This is one of Italy's finest wines and is a full-bodied red. Serve with rich meaty dishes, game or spicy sausage pasta sauces.

Chianti This wine is best drunk when young and may be served slightly chilled. It is often regarded as the classic accompaniment to pasta.

Pasta Equipment

When making and cooking pasta, a bare minimum of equipment is needed; some would say that a rolling pin, a large pan and a colander would suffice, however, there are many gadgets that make the process a lot easier.

When Making
Rolling pin Try to use one that is quite slender and choose a conventional wooden one without handles. In Italy pasta rolling pins are very long, for rolling out large quantities of pasta at a time, and slightly thicker in the middle with tapering ends.

Pasta machine A traditional, hand-cranked pasta machine has adjusting rollers and usually cutters for making tagliatelle and finer tagliarini. More complicated ones come with a selection of cutters.

Pasta wheel This is useful for cutting noodles such as tagliatelle and pappardelle if you do not have a pasta machine and also for stuffed shapes such as ravioli. This is an inexpensive piece of equipment and less likely to drag or tear the pasta than a knife.

Ravioli cutter Specially designed, fluted-edged cutters can be bought for cutting pasta. A fluted or plain biscuit cutter works just as well.

When Cooking and Serving
Long-handled pasta fork This is useful for stirring the pasta to keep the pieces separate during cooking. You can also get wooden pasta hooks which will lift out the strands of pasta so that you can check whether or not it is cooked.

Parmesan graters These range from simple hand graters to electrical gadgets. If sharp, the fine side of a box grater works equally well.

Parmesan knife This is used to shave Parmesan off a block. A vegetable peeler may be used as an alternative.

Pasta cooking pot Officially this should be tall with straight sides and handles and should have an inner basket. When buying, choose one that is not too heavy, and will be easy to manage when full.

Pasta measurer This is a wooden gadget with several holes for measuring spaghetti. Each hole takes a different amount of pasta for a given number of people.

Cooking Techniques for Potatoes

Generally, new potato varieties have a firm and waxy texture that do not break up during cooking, so are ideal for boiling, steaming and salads. Main crop potatoes, on the other hand, have a more floury texture and lend themselves to mashing and roasting – both types are suitable for chips. When cooking potatoes, it is important to make sure the potatoes that you are using are the correct type for the dish being prepared. Whichever way you choose to serve potatoes, allow 175–225 g/6–8 oz per person.

Boiling Potatoes
New Potatoes

Most of the new potatoes available nowadays are fairly clean – especially those sold in supermarkets – and simply need a light scrub before cooking in their skins. If the potatoes are very dirty, use a small scrubbing brush or scourer to remove both the skins and dirt. Add them to a pan of cold, salted water and bring to the boil. Cover the pan with a lid and simmer for 12–15 minutes or until tender. Add a couple of sprigs of fresh herbs to the pan if you like – fresh mint is traditionally used to flavour potatoes. Drain the potatoes thoroughly and

serve hot, tossed in a little melted butter or, for a change, a tablespoon of pesto. The skins of first early new potatoes will peel away easily, but second earlies should be served in their skins or peeled when cooked – hold the hot potatoes with a fork to make this easier. Very firm new potatoes can be added to boiling water, simmered for 8 minutes, and then left to stand in the hot water for a further 10 minutes until cooked through.

Old Potatoes

Choose a main crop potato suitable for boiling, then thinly peel and cut into even-sized pieces. Add to a saucepan of cold, salted water and bring to the boil. Cover the pan with a lid and simmer for 20 minutes or until tender.

Alternatively, you can cook the potatoes in their skins and peel them after cooking. It is particularly important to cook floury potatoes gently or the outsides may start to fall apart before they are tender in the centre. Drain the potatoes in a colander, then return them to the pan to dry out over a very low heat for 1–2 minutes. If you are planning to serve the potatoes mashed, roughly mash them and add a knob of butter and

2 tablespoons of milk per person. Mash until smooth, either with a hand masher, mouli grater or a potato ricer. Season to taste with salt, freshly ground black pepper and a little freshly grated nutmeg if liked, then beat for a few seconds with a wooden spoon until fluffy. As an alternative to butter, use a good quality olive oil or crème fraîche. Finely chopped red and green chillies, crispy-cooked crumbled bacon, fresh herbs or grated Parmesan cheese can also be stirred in for additional flavour.

Steaming Potatoes

All potatoes are suitable for steaming. Floury potatoes, however, are ideal for this method of cooking as they fall apart easily.

New and small potatoes can be steamed whole, but larger ones should be cut into even-sized pieces. Place the potatoes in a steamer, colander or sieve over boiling water and cover. Steam for 10 minutes if the potatoes are very small or if they are cut into large chunks cook for 20–25 minutes.

Frying Potatoes
Chipped Potatoes

To make chips, wash, peel and cut the potatoes into 1.5 cm/½ inch slices. Cut the slices into long strips also about 1.5 cm/½ inch wide. Place the strips in a bowl of cold water and leave for 20 minutes, then drain and dry well on kitchen paper – moisture will make the fat spit. Pour some oil into a deep, heavy based saucepan or deep-fat fryer, making sure that the oil does not go any further than halfway up the sides of the pan. Heat the oil to 190°C/375°F, or until a chip dropped into the fat rises to the surface straight away and is surrounded by bubbles. Put the chips into a wire basket and lower into the oil and cook for 7–8 minutes or until golden. Remove and increase the heat of the oil to 200°C/400°F. Lower the chips into the oil again and cook for 2–3 minutes, or until they are crisp and golden brown. Drain on kitchen paper before serving.

Slightly finer chips are properly known as *pommes frites*, even finer ones as *pommes allumettes* and the finest of all as *pommes pailles* (straw chips). Paper-thin slices of peeled potatoes, cut with a sharp knife or using a mandoline or food processor, can be deep-fried a few at a time to make crisps or game chips.

Healthy Chips

To make lower-fat chips, preheat the oven to 200°C/400°F/Gas Mark 6 and place a non-stick baking tray in the oven to heat up. Cut the potatoes into chips as above or into chunky wedges, if preferred. Put the chips or wedges in a pan of cold water and quickly bring to the boil. Simmer for 2 minutes, then drain in a colander. Leave for a few minutes to dry, then drizzle over 1½–2 tablespoons of olive or sunflower oil and toss to coat. Tip on to the heated baking tray and cook in the preheated oven for 20–25 minutes, turning occasionally until golden brown and crisp.

Sauteed Potatoes

Cut peeled potatoes into rounds about 0.5 cm/¼ inch thick and pat dry. Heat 25 g/1 oz unsalted butter and 2 tablespoons of oil in a large, heavy based frying pan until hot. Add the potatoes in a single layer and cook for 4–5 minutes until the undersides are golden. Turn with a large fish slice and cook the other side until golden and tender. Drain on kitchen paper and sprinkle with a little salt before serving.

Baking Potatoes

Allow a 300–350 g/11–12 oz potato per person and choose a variety such as Maris Piper, Cara or King Edward. Wash and dry the potatoes, prick the skins lightly, then rub each one with a little oil and sprinkle with salt. Bake at 200°C/400°F/Gas Mark 6 for 1–1½ hours or until the skins are

crisp and the centres are very soft. To speed up the cooking time, thread on to metal skewers as this conducts heat to the middle of the potatoes.

Roasting Potatoes

For crisp and brown outsides and fluffy centres choose potatoes suitable for baking. Thinly peel the potatoes and cut into even-sized pieces. Drop them into a pan of boiling, salted water and simmer for 5 minutes. Turn off the heat and leave for a further 3–4 minutes. Drain well and return the potatoes to the pan over a low heat for a minute to dry them and to roughen the edges. Carefully transfer them to a roasting tin containing hot oil or dripping. Baste well, then bake at 220°C/425°F/ Gas Mark 7 for 20 minutes. Turn them and cook for a further 20–30 minutes, turning and basting at least one more time. Serve as soon as the potatoes are ready.

Potato Croquettes

Mash dry, boiled potatoes with just a little butter or olive oil, then stir in 1 egg yolk mixed with 1–2 tablespoons of milk or crème fraîche to make a firm mixture. Shape the mashed potatoes into small cylinders about 5 cm/2 inches long, rolling them in flour. Dip in beaten egg and then in fresh, white breadcrumbs. Chill the croquettes in the refrigerator for 30 minutes. Place a little unsalted butter and oil in a heavy-based frying pan and slowly heat until the butter has melted. Shallow fry the croquettes, turning occasionally until they are golden brown and crisp.

Rosti

Parboil peeled, waxy potatoes in boiling, salted water for 8 minutes, then drain and leave to cool before coarsely grating into a bowl. Season well with salt and freshly ground black pepper and freshly chopped herbs if liked. Heat a mixture of unsalted butter and oil in a heavy based frying pan until bubbling. Add tablespoonfuls

of the grated potato into the pan and flatten with the back of a fish slice. Cook over a medium heat for about 7 minutes or until crisp and golden. Turn and cook the other side, then serve while still hot.

Cooking Potatoes in a Clay Pot

Terracotta potato pots can cook up to 450 g/1 lb of whole potatoes at a time. Soak the clay pot for at least 20 minutes before use, then add even-sized, preferably smallish potatoes. Drizzle over a little olive oil and season generously with salt and freshly ground black pepper. Cover the pot with the lid and put in a cold oven, setting the temperature to 200°C/400°F/Gas Mark 6. The potatoes will take about 45 minutes to cook.

Microwaved Potatoes

This method of cooking is suitable for boiling and baking potatoes, providing you do not want the skins to be crispy. To cook new potatoes, prick the skins with a skewer to prevent them from bursting, then place in a bowl with 3 tablespoons of boiling water. Cover with clingfilm which has been pierced two or three times and cook on high for 12–15 minutes, or until tender. Peeled chunks of potato can be cooked in the same way. To bake potatoes, place each potato on a circle of kitchen paper. Make several cuts in each to ensure that the skins do not burst. Transfer to the microwave plate and cook on high for 4–6 minutes per potato, allowing an extra 3–4 minutes for every additional potato. Turn the potatoes at least once during cooking. Leave to stand for 5 minutes before serving.

Health and Nutrition

Potatoes are high in complex carbohydrates, providing sustained energy. They are also an excellent source of vitamins B and C and minerals such as iron and potassium. They contain almost no fat and are high in dietary fibre.

Cooking Techniques for Rice

There are countless ways to cook rice and there are even more opinions about how to do so! Much, of course, depends on the variety and brand of rice being used, the dish being prepared and the desired results. Each variety of rice has its own characteristics. Some types of rice cook to light, separate grains; some to a rich, creamy consistency; and some to a consistency where the grains stick together. It is important, therefore, to ensure that the appropriate rice is used. Different types of rice have very different powers of absorption. Long-grain rice will absorb about three times its weight in water, whereas just 25 g/1 oz of plump and short-grained pudding rice can soak up a massive 300 ml/½ pint of liquid.

Cooking Long-grain Rice

By far the simplest method of cooking long-grain rice – whether white, brown or basmati – is to add it to plenty of boiling, salted water in a large saucepan, so that the rice grains can move freely and do not stick together. Allow about 50 g/2 oz of rice per person when cooking as an accompaniment. Rinse it under cold, running water until clear – this removes any starch still clinging to the grains – then tip into the rapidly boiling water. Stir once, then when the water comes back to the boil, turn down the heat a little and simmer uncovered, allowing 10–12 minutes for white rice and 30–40 minutes for brown (check the packet timings, as brands of rice vary). The easiest way to test if the rice is cooked is to bite a couple of grains – they should be tender but still firm. Drain the rice straight away, then return to the pan with a little butter and herbs if liked. Fluff the grains with a fork and serve. If you need to keep the rice warm, put it in a bowl and place over a pan of barely simmering water. Cover the top of the bowl with a clean tea towel until ready to serve.

Absorption Method

Cooking rice using the absorption method is also very simple and is favoured by many because no draining is involved and therefore no water is wasted. Also, by using this method, stock and other flavourful ingredients can be added and will be absorbed by the rice. Furthermore, valuable nutrients are retained that would otherwise be lost in the cooking water when drained. To cook rice this way, weigh out the quantity of rice you require, then measure it by volume in a measuring jug – you will need about 150 ml/¼ pint for two people. Briefly rinse the rice in a sieve under cold running water, then tip into a large heavy based saucepan. If liked, you can cook the rice in a little butter or oil for about 1 minute. Pour in two parts water to one part rice (or use stock if you prefer), season with salt and bring to the boil uncovered. Cover the pan with a tight-fitting lid, then simmer gently without lifting the lid, until the liquid is absorbed and the rice is tender. White rice will take 15 minutes to cook, whereas brown rice will take about 35 minutes. It is important to simmer over a very low heat or the liquid will cook away before the rice is ready. Do not be tempted to check the rice too often while it is cooking as you will let out steam and therefore moisture. If there is still a little liquid left when the rice is tender, remove the lid and cook for about a minute until evaporated. Remove from the heat and leave to stand with the lid on for 4–5 minutes. Do not rinse the rice when it is cooked, just fluff up with a fork before serving. This method is also good for cooking Jasmine and Valencia rice.

Oven-baked Method

The oven-baked method also works by absorption. It takes a little longer than cooking rice on the hob, but is ideal to add to the oven if you are roasting or simmering a casserole.

To make oven-baked rice for two people, gently fry a chopped onion in 1 tablespoon of olive oil in a 1.1 litre/2 pint flameproof casserole dish until soft and golden (leave the onion out if preferred). Add 75 g/3 oz long-grain rice and cook for 1 minute, then stir in 300 ml/½ pint of stock – you can also add a finely pared strip of lemon rind or a bay leaf at this stage. Cover with a lid or tinfoil and bake on the middle shelf of a preheated oven at

180°C/350°F/Gas Mark 4 for 40 minutes, or until the rice is tender and all the stock has been absorbed. Fluff up with a fork before serving.

Cooking in the Microwave

Rinse long-grain white or brown rice in cold running water, then place in a large heat-proof bowl. Add boiling water or stock to the bowl, allowing 300 ml/ $\frac{1}{2}$ pint for 125 g/4 oz rice and 550 ml/ 18 fl oz for 225 g/8 oz rice. Add a pinch of salt and a knob of butter, if desired. Cover with clingfilm, making a few air holes to allow the steam to escape and microwave on high for 3 minutes. Stir, then re-cover and microwave on medium for 12 minutes for white rice and 25 minutes for brown. Leave to stand, covered, for 5 minutes before fluffing up with a fork and serving.

In a Pressure Cooker

Follow the quantities given for the absorption method and bring to the boil in the pressure cooker. Stir once, cover with the lid and bring to a high 6.8 kg/15 lb pressure. Lower the heat and cook for 5 minutes if white rice or cook for 8 minutes if brown rice.

In a Rice Cooker

Follow the quantities given for the absorption method. Put the rice, salt and boiling water or stock in the cooker, bring back to the boil and cover. When all the liquid has been absorbed the cooker will turn itself off automatically.

Wild Rice

This type of rice can be cooked by any of the methods used for long-grain rice, but the cooking time required is longer. It will take between 35–50 minutes to cook wild rice, depending on whether you like your rice slightly chewy or very tender. To speed up the cooking time by 5–10 minutes, soak the rice in cold water first for 30 minutes. This also increases the volume of the rice when it is cooked.

Red Rice

Cook this in the same way as brown rice as this type of rice has a very hard grain. It is best to cook the rice for about 40–60 minutes if you like your rice really tender – it will still keep its shape.

Risotto Rice

Most rices should not be stirred during cooking as it breaks up the grains and makes them soggy. Risotto rice is different as it can absorb nearly five times its weight in liquid and still retains its shape. A good risotto has a creamy texture, with a slight bite to the individual grains and is made by adding the cooking liquid gradually and stirring almost continuously during cooking.

For a classic risotto (known as *alla Milanese*) for four people, place 1 tablespoon of olive oil and a knob of butter in a large heavy based saucepan. Slowly heat the butter and oil until the butter has melted. Add 1 chopped onion to the pan and cook until tender. Add 150 ml/ $\frac{1}{4}$ pint of dry white wine and boil rapidly until almost totally reduced. Stir in 300 g/11 oz risotto rice. Add 1 litre/ $1\frac{3}{4}$ pints boiling vegetable or chicken stock, a ladleful at a time – each ladleful should be completely absorbed by the rice before the next one is added. Continue adding the stock until the rice is tender. This will take 15–20 minutes, although it may not be necessary to add all of the stock to achieve the desired consistency. Serve the risotto straight away, sprinkled with grated Parmesan cheese. The basic risotto can be flavoured in many ways. Try adding a couple of bay leaves, a lemon grass stalk or a large pinch of saffron to the stock, or use more red or white wine and less stock.

Glutinous Rice

This rice is steamed (instead of being cooked in boiling water) until the grains are soft, tender and stick together in a mass. Cooking times vary slightly according to the brand, so check the packet instructions for specific directions.

Pudding Rice

For a simple rice pudding put 50 g/ 2 oz of pudding rice in a buttered 1.2 litre/2 pint ovenproof dish with sugar to taste. Pour over 600 ml/1 pint of near-boiling milk and bake in a preheated oven at 150°C/300°F/Gas Mark 2 for 30 minutes. Stir, then bake for a further 1–1 $\frac{1}{4}$ hours until tender. Vary the flavour by infusing the milk with orange rind, adding nuts and dried fruit to the mixture or using 300 ml/ $\frac{1}{2}$ pint coconut milk or single cream and 300 ml/ $\frac{1}{2}$ pint of milk instead of milk alone.

Health and Nutrition

Rice has been the dietary staple of the East for centuries where it has provided a healthy, balanced diet and has added substance to the small quantities of meat used in Eastern cooking. It is low in fat and high in complex carbohydrates which are absorbed slowly, helping to maintain blood sugar levels. Rice is also a reasonable source of protein and provides most of the B vitamins and the minerals potassium and phosphorus. It is also a gluten-free cereal, making it suitable for coeliacs. Like other unrefined grains, brown rice is richer in nutrients and fibre than refined white rice.

Herbs and Spices

Herbs are easy to grow and a garden is not needed as they can easily thrive on a small patio, window box or even on a windowsill. It is worth the effort to plant a few herbs as they do not require much attention or nurturing. The reward will be a range of fresh herbs available whenever needed, and fresh flavours that cannot be beaten to add to any dish that is being prepared.

While fresh herbs should be picked or bought as close as possible to the time of use, freeze-dried and dried herbs and spices will usually keep for around six months.

The best idea is to buy little and often, and to store the herbs in airtight jars in a cool dark cupboard. Fresh herbs tend to have a milder flavour than dried and equate to around one level tablespoon of fresh to one level teaspoon of dried. As a result, quantities used in cooking should be altered accordingly. A variety of herbs and spices and their uses are listed below.

ALLSPICE
The dark allspice berries come whole or ground and have a flavour similar to that of cinnamon, cloves and nutmeg. Although not the same as mixed spices, allspice can be used with pickles, relishes, cakes and milk puddings or whole in meat and fish dishes.

ANISEED
Aniseed comes in whole seeds or ground. It has a strong aroma and flavour and should be used sparingly in baking and salad dressings.

BASIL
Best fresh but also available in dried form, basil can be used raw or cooked. It works well in many dishes but is particularly well suited to tomato-based dishes and sauces, salads and Mediterranean recipes.

BAY LEAVES
Bay leaves are available in fresh or dried form as well as ground. They make up part of a bouquet garni and are particularly delicious when added to meat and poultry dishes, soups, stews, vegetable dishes and stuffing. They also impart a spicy flavour to milk puddings and egg custards.

BOUQUET GARNI
Bouquet garni is a bouquet of fresh herbs tied with a piece of string or in a small piece of muslin. It is used to flavour casseroles, stews and stocks or sauces. The herbs that are normally used are parsley, thyme, and bay leaves.

CARAWAY SEEDS
Caraway seeds have a warm sweet taste and are often used in breads and cakes but are delicious with cabbage dishes and pickles as well.

CAYENNE
Cayenne is the powdered form of a red chilli pepper said to be native to Cayenne. It is similar in appearance to paprika and can be used sparingly to add a fiery kick to many dishes.

CARDAMOM
Cardamom has a distinctive sweet, rich taste and can be bought whole in the pod, in seed form or ground. This sweet aromatic spice is delicious in curries, rice, cakes and biscuits and is great served with rice pudding and fruit.

CHERVIL
Reminiscent of parsley and available either in fresh or dried form, chervil has a faintly sweet, spicy flavour and is particularly good in soups, cheese dishes, stews and with eggs.

CHILLI
Available whole, fresh, dried and in powdered form, red chillies tend to be sweeter in taste than their green counterparts. They are particularly associated with Spanish and Mexican-style cooking and curries, but are also delicious with pickles, dips, sauces and in pizza toppings.

CHIVES
Best used when fresh but also available in dried form, this member of the onion family is ideal for use when a delicate onion flavour is required. Chives are good with eggs, cheese, fish and vegetable dishes. They also work well as a garnish for soups, meat and vegetable dishes.

CINNAMON
Cinnamon comes in the form of reddish-brown sticks of bark from an evergreen tree and has a sweet, pungent aroma. Either whole or ground, cinnamon is delicious in cakes and milk puddings, particularly with apple, and is used in mulled wine and for preserving.

CLOVES
Mainly used whole although also available ground, cloves have a very warm, sweet pungent aroma and can be used to stud roast ham and pork, in mulled wine and punch and when pickling fruit. When ground, they can be used in making mincemeat and in Christmas puddings and biscuits.

CORIANDER
Coriander seeds have an orangey flavour and are available whole or ground. Coriander is particularly delicious (whether whole or roughly ground) in casseroles, curries and as a pickling spice. The leaves are used to flavour spicy aromatic dishes as well as a garnish.

CUMIN
Also available ground or as whole seeds, cumin has a strong, slightly bitter flavour. It is one of the main ingredients in curry powder and compliments many fish, meat and rice dishes.

DILL
Dill leaves are available fresh or dried and have a mild flavour, while the seeds are slightly bitter. Dill is particularly good with salmon, new potatoes and in sauces. The seeds are good in pickles and vegetable dishes.

FENNEL
Whole seeds or ground, fennel has a fragrant, sweet aniseed flavour and is sometimes known as the fish herb because it compliments fish dishes so well.

GINGER
Ginger comes in many forms but primarily as a fresh root and in dried ground form, which can be used in baking, curries, pickles, sauces and Chinese cooking.

LEMON GRASS
Available fresh and dried, with a subtle, aromatic, lemony flavour, lemon grass is essential to Thai cooking. It is also delicious when added to soups, poultry and fish dishes.

MACE

The outer husk of nutmeg has a milder nutmeg flavour and can be used in pickles, cheese dishes, stewed fruits, sauces and hot punch.

MARJORAM
Often dried, marjoram has a sweet slightly spicy flavour, which tastes fantastic when added to stuffing, meat or tomato-based dishes.

MINT
Available fresh or dried, mint has a strong, sweet aroma which is delicious in a sauce or jelly to serve with lamb. It is also great with fresh peas and new potatoes and is an essential ingredient in Pimms.

MUSTARD SEED
These yellow and brown seeds are available whole or ground and are often found in pickles, relishes, cheese dishes, dressings, curries and as an accompaniment to meat.

NUTMEG
The large whole seeds have a warm, sweet taste and compliment custards, milk puddings, cheese dishes, parsnips and creamy soups.

OREGANO
The strongly flavoured dried leaves of oregano are similar to marjoram and are used extensively in Italian and Greek cooking.

PAPRIKA
Paprika often comes in two varieties. One is quite sweet and mild and the other has a slight bite to it. Paprika is made from the fruit of the sweet pepper and is good in meat and poultry dishes as well as a garnish. The rule of buying herbs and spices little and often applies particularly to paprika as unfortunately it does not keep particularly well.

PARSLEY
The stems as well as the leaves of parsley can be used to compliment most savoury dishes as they contain the most flavour. They can also be used as a garnish.

PEPPER
This comes in white and black peppercorns and is best freshly ground. Both add flavour to most dishes, sauces and gravies. Black pepper has a more robust flavour, while white pepper is much more delicate.

POPPY SEEDS
These tiny, grey-black coloured seeds impart a sweet, nutty flavour when added to biscuits, vegetable dishes, dressings and cheese dishes.

ROSEMARY
Delicious fresh or dried, these small, needle-like leaves have a sweet aroma which is particularly good with lamb, stuffing and vegetable dishes. Also delicious when added to charcoal on the barbecue to give a piquant flavour to meat and corn on the cob.

SAFFRON
Deep orange in colour, saffron is traditionally used in paella, rice and cakes but is also delicious with poultry. Saffron is the most expensive of all spices.

SAGE
Fresh or dried sage leaves have a pungent, slightly bitter taste which is delicious with pork and poultry, sausages, stuffing and with stuffed pasta when tossed in a little butter and fresh sage.

SAVORY
This herb resembles thyme, but has a softer flavour that particularly compliments all types of fish and beans.

SESAME
Sesame seeds have a nutty taste, especially when toasted, and are delicious in baking, on salads, or with Far-Eastern cooking.

TARRAGON
The fresh or dried leaves of tarragon have a sweet aromatic taste which is particularly good with poultry, seafood, fish, creamy sauces and stuffing.

THYME
Available fresh or dried, thyme has a pungent flavour and is included in bouquet garni. It compliments many meat and poultry dishes and stuffing.

TURMERIC
Turmeric is obtained from the root of a lily from southeast Asia. This root is ground and has a brilliant yellow colour. It has a bitter, peppery flavour and is often combined for use in curry powder and mustard. Also delicious in pickles, relishes and dressings.

Potato & Fennel Soup

INGREDIENTS

Serves 4

25 g/1 oz butter
2 large onions, peeled
  and thinly sliced
2–3 garlic cloves, peeled and crushed
1 tsp salt
2 medium potatoes (about
  450 g/1 lb in weight), peeled
  and diced
1 fennel bulb, trimmed and
  finely chopped
½ tsp caraway seeds
1 litre/1¾ pints vegetable stock
freshly ground black pepper
2 tbsp freshly chopped parsley
4 tbsp crème fraîche
roughly torn pieces of French stick,
  to serve

FOOD FACT

A fennel bulb is in fact the swollen stem of a plant known as Florence fennel. Originating in Italy, Florence fennel has a distinct aniseed flavour, which mellows and sweetens when cooked. Look out for well rounded bulbs with bright green fronds.

1 Melt the butter in a large heavy-based saucepan. Add the onions, with the garlic and half the salt, and cook over a medium heat, stirring occasionally, for 7–10 minutes, or until the onions are very soft and beginning to turn brown.

2 Add the potatoes, fennel bulb, caraway seeds and the remaining salt. Cook for about 5 minutes, then pour in the vegetable stock. Bring to the boil, partially cover and simmer for 15–20 minutes, or until the potatoes are tender. Stir in the chopped parsley and adjust the seasoning to taste.

3 For a smooth-textured soup, allow to cool slightly then pour into a food processor or blender and blend until smooth. Reheat the soup gently, then ladle into individual soup bowls. For a chunky soup, omit this blending stage and ladle straight from the saucepan into soup bowls.

4 Swirl a spoonful of crème fraîche into each bowl and serve immediately with roughly torn pieces of French stick.

Rocket & Potato Soup with Garlic Croûtons

INGREDIENTS

Serves 4

700 g/1½ lb baby new potatoes
1.1 litres/2 pints chicken or
 vegetable stock
50 g/2 oz rocket leaves
125 g/4 oz thick white
 sliced bread
50 g/2 oz unsalted butter
1 tsp groundnut oil
2–4 garlic cloves, peeled
 and chopped
125 g/4 oz stale ciabatta bread,
 with the crusts removed
4 tbsp olive oil
salt and freshly ground black pepper
2 tbsp Parmesan cheese,
 finely grated

1 Place the potatoes in a large saucepan, cover with the stock and simmer gently for 10 minutes. Add the rocket leaves and simmer for a further 5–10 minutes, or until the potatoes are soft and the rocket has wilted.

2 Meanwhile, make the croûtons. Cut the thick white sliced bread into small cubes and reserve. Heat the butter and groundnut oil in a small frying pan and cook the garlic for 1 minute, stirring well. Remove the garlic. Add the bread cubes to the butter and oil mixture in the frying pan and sauté, stirring continuously, until they are golden brown. Drain the croûtons on absorbent kitchen paper and reserve.

3 Cut the ciabatta bread into small dice and stir into the soup. Cover the saucepan and leave to stand for 10 minutes, or until the bread has absorbed a lot of the liquid.

4 Stir in the olive oil, season to taste with salt and pepper and serve at once with a few of the garlic croûtons scattered over the top and a little grated Parmesan cheese.

HELPFUL HINT

Rocket is now widely available in bags from most large supermarkets. If, however, you cannot get hold of it, replace it with an equal quantity of watercress or baby spinach leaves.

1

2

3

Carrot & Ginger Soup

INGREDIENTS

Serves 4

4 slices of bread, crusts removed
1 tsp yeast extract
2 tsp olive oil
1 onion, peeled and chopped
1 garlic clove, peeled and crushed
½ tsp ground ginger
450 g/1 lb carrots, peeled
  and chopped
1 litre/1¾ pint vegetable stock
2.5 cm/1 inch piece of
  root ginger, peeled and finely grated
salt and freshly ground
  black pepper
1 tbsp lemon juice

To garnish:
chives
lemon zest

1 Preheat the oven to 180°C/350°F/Gas Mark 4. Roughly chop the bread. Dissolve the yeast extract in 2 tablespoons of warm water and mix with the bread.

2 Spread the bread cubes over a lightly oiled baking tray and bake for 20 minutes, turning halfway through. Remove from the oven and reserve.

3 Heat the oil in a large saucepan. Gently cook the onion and garlic for 3–4 minutes.

4 Stir in the ground ginger and cook for 1 minute to release the flavour.

5 Add the chopped carrots, then stir in the stock and the fresh ginger. Simmer gently for 15 minutes.

6 Remove from the heat and allow to cool a little. Blend until smooth, then season to taste with salt and pepper. Stir in the lemon juice. Garnish with the chives and lemon zest and serve immediately.

2

4

6

Balsamic Strawberries with Mascarpone

INGREDIENTS

Serves 4–6

450 g/1 lb fresh strawberries

2–3 tbsp best-quality
balsamic vinegar

freshly ground black pepper

fresh mint leaves, torn, plus
extra to decorate (optional)

115–175 g/4–6 oz mascarpone cheese

1 Wipe the strawberries with a damp cloth, rather than rinsing them, so they do not become soggy. Using a paring knife, cut off the green stalks at the top and use the tip of the knife to remove the core.

2 Cut each strawberry in half lengthways, or into quarters if large. Transfer to a bowl.

3 Add the vinegar, allowing ½ tablespoon per person. Add several twists of ground black pepper, then gently stir together. Cover with clingfilm and chill for up to 4 hours.

4 Just before serving, stir in torn mint leaves to taste. Spoon the mascarpone cheese into individual bowls and spoon the berries on top. Decorate with a few mint leaves, if wished. Sprinkle with extra pepper to taste.

HELPFUL HINT

This is most enjoyable when it is made with the best-quality balsamic vinegar, one that has aged slowly and has turned thick and syrupy. Unfortunately, the genuine mixture is always expensive. Less expensive versions are artificially sweetened and coloured with caramel, or taste of harsh vinegar.

1

3

4

Fish Soup Provençale

INGREDIENTS

Serves 4–6

1 tbsp olive oil

2 onions, finely chopped

1 small leek, thinly sliced

1 small carrot, finely chopped

1 stalk celery, finely chopped

1 small fennel bulb, finely
  chopped (optional)

3 garlic cloves, finely chopped

225 ml/8 fl oz dry white wine

1.2 litres/2 pints water

400 g/14 oz can tomatoes in juice

1 bay leaf

pinch of fennel seeds

2 strips orange rind

¼ tsp saffron threads

350 g/12 oz skinless white
  fish fillets

salt and pepper

garlic croûtons, to serve

1. Heat the oil in a large saucepan over a medium heat. Add the onions and cook for about 5 minutes, stirring frequently, until softened. Add the leek, carrot, celery, fennel and garlic and continue cooking for 4–5 minutes until the leek is wilted.

2. Add the wine and let it bubble for a minute. Add the tomatoes, bay leaf, fennel seeds, orange rind, saffron and water. Bring just to the boil, reduce the heat, cover and cook gently, stirring occasionally, for 30 minutes.

3. Add the fish and cook for a further 20–30 minutes until it is very soft and flaky. Remove the bay leaf and orange rind if possible.

4. Allow the soup to cool slightly, then transfer to a blender or food processor and purée until smooth, working in batches if necessary. (If using a food processor, strain off the cooking liquid and reserve. Purée the soup solids with enough cooking liquid to moisten them, then combine with the remaining liquid.)

5. Return the soup to the saucepan. Taste and adjust the seasoning, if necessary, and simmer for 5–10 minutes until heated through. Ladle the soup into warm bowls and sprinkle with croûtons.

Pumpkin & Smoked Haddock Soup

INGREDIENTS

Serves 4–6

2 tbsp olive oil

1 medium onion, peeled and chopped

2 garlic cloves, peeled and chopped

3 celery stalks, trimmed and chopped

700 g/1½ lb pumpkin, peeled, deseeded and cut into chunks

450 g/1 lb potatoes, peeled and cut into chunks

750 ml/1¼ pints chicken stock, heated

125 ml/4 fl oz dry sherry

200 g/7 oz smoked haddock fillet

150 ml/¼ pint milk

freshly ground black pepper

2 tbsp freshly chopped parsley

1 Heat the oil in a large heavy-based saucepan and gently cook the onion, garlic, and celery for about 10 minutes. This will release the sweetness but not colour the vegetables. Add the pumpkin and potatoes to the saucepan and stir to coat the vegetables with the oil.

2 Gradually pour in the stock and bring to the boil. Cover, then reduce the heat and simmer for 25 minutes, stirring occasionally. Stir in the dry sherry, then remove the saucepan from the heat and leave to cool for 5–10 minutes.

3 Blend the mixture in a food processor or blender to form a chunky purée and return to the cleaned saucepan.

4 Meanwhile, place the fish in a shallow frying pan. Pour in the milk with 3 tablespoons of water and bring to almost boiling point. Reduce the heat, cover and simmer for 6 minutes, or until the fish is cooked and flakes easily. Remove from the heat and, using a slotted spoon remove the fish from the liquid, reserving both liquid and fish.

5 Discard the skin and any bones from the fish and flake into pieces. Stir the fish liquid into the soup, together with the flaked fish. Season with freshly ground black pepper, stir in the parsley and serve immediately.

TASTY TIP

Try to find undyed smoked haddock for this soup rather than the brightly coloured yellow type, as the texture and flavour is better.

Creamy Salmon with Dill in Filo Baskets

INGREDIENTS

Serves 4

1 bay leaf
6 black peppercorns
1 large sprig fresh parsley
175 g/6 oz salmon fillet
4 large sheets filo pastry
fine spray of oil
125 g/4 oz baby spinach leaves
8 tbsp low-fat fromage frais
2 tsp Dijon mustard
2 tbsp freshly chopped dill
salt and freshly ground
  black pepper

1 Preheat the oven to 200°C/400°F/Gas Mark 6. Place the bay leaf, peppercorns, parsley and salmon in a frying pan and add enough water to barely cover the fish.

2 Bring to the boil, reduce the heat and poach the fish for 5 minutes until it flakes easily. Remove it from the pan. Reserve.

3 Spray each sheet of filo pastry lightly with the oil. Scrunch up the pastry to make a nest shape approximately 12.5 cm/5 inches in diameter.

4 Place on a lightly oiled baking sheet and cook in the preheated oven for 10 minutes until golden and crisp.

5 Blanch the spinach in a pan of lightly salted boiling water for 2 minutes. Drain thoroughly and keep warm.

6 Mix the fromage frais, mustard and dill together, then warm gently. Season to taste with salt and pepper. Divide the spinach between the filo pastry nests and flake the salmon onto the spinach.

7 Spoon the mustard and dill sauce over the filo baskets and serve immediately.

FOOD FACT

This is a highly nutritious dish combining calcium-rich salmon with vitamin- and mineral-rich spinach. The low-fat fromage frais in this recipe can be substituted with low-fat live yogurt if you want to aid digestion and give the immune system a real boost!

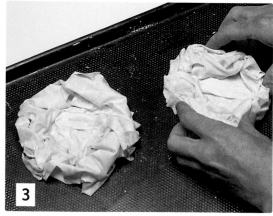

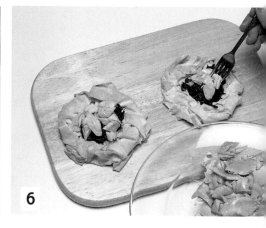

Griddled Garlic & Lemon Squid

INGREDIENTS

Serves 4

125 g/4 oz long-grain rice
300 ml/½ pint fish stock
225 g/8 oz squid, cleaned
finely grated rind of 1 lemon
1 garlic clove, peeled
   and crushed
1 shallot, peeled and
   finely chopped
2 tbsp freshly
   chopped coriander
2 tbsp lemon juice
salt and freshly ground
   black pepper

HELPFUL HINT

To prepare squid, peel the tentacles from the squid's pouch and cut away the head just below the eye. Discard the head. Remove the quill and the soft innards from the squid and discard. Peel off any dark skin that covers the squid and discard. Rinse the tentacles and pouch thoroughly. The squid is now ready to use.

1 Rinse the rice until the water runs clear, then place in a saucepan with the stock.

2 Bring to the boil, then reduce the heat. Cover and simmer gently for 10 minutes.

3 Turn off the heat and leave the pan covered so the rice can steam while you cook the squid.

4 Remove the tentacles from the squid and reserve.

5 Cut the body cavity in half. Using the tip of a small sharp knife, score the inside flesh of the body cavity in a diamond pattern. Do not cut all the way through.

6 Mix the lemon rind, crushed garlic and chopped shallot together.

7 Place the squid in a shallow bowl and sprinkle over the lemon mixture and stir.

8 Heat a griddle pan until almost smoking. Cook the squid for 3–4 minutes until cooked through, then slice.

9 Sprinkle with the coriander and lemon juice. Season to taste with salt and pepper. Drain the rice and serve immediately with the squid.

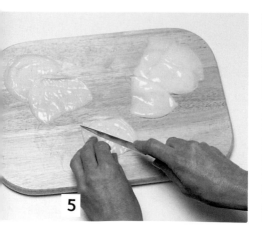

5

7

8

Garlic Fish Soup

INGREDIENTS

Serves 4

2 tsp olive oil

1 large onion, chopped

1 small fennel bulb, chopped

1 leek, sliced

3–4 large garlic cloves, thinly sliced

120 ml / 4 fl oz dry white wine

1.2 litres/2 pints fish stock

4 tbsp white rice

1 strip pared lemon rind

1 bay leaf

450 g/1 lb skinless white fish fillets,
   cut into 4 cm/1½ inch pieces

50 ml/2 fl oz double cream

2 tbsp fresh parsley, chopped

salt and pepper

1 Heat the oil in a large saucepan over a medium-low heat. Add the onion, fennel, leek and garlic and cook for 4–5 minutes, stirring frequently, until the onion is softened.

2 Add the wine and bubble briefly. Add the stock, rice, lemon rind and bay leaf. Bring to the boil, reduce the heat to medium-low and simmer for 20–25 minutes, or until the rice and vegetables are soft. Remove the lemon rind and bay leaf.

3 Allow the soup to cool slightly, then transfer to a blender or food processor and purée until smooth, working in batches if necessary. (If using a food processor, strain off the cooking liquid and reserve. Purée the soup solids with enough cooking liquid to moisten them, then combine with the remaining liquid.)

4 Return the soup to the saucepan and bring to a simmer. Add the fish to the soup, cover and continue simmering gently, stirring occasionally, for 4–5 minutes, or until the fish is cooked and begins to flake.

5 Stir in the cream. Taste and adjust the seasoning, adding salt, if needed, and pepper. Ladle into warmed bowls and serve sprinkled with parsley.

1

2

4

Smoked Salmon Sushi

INGREDIENTS

Serves 4

175 g/6 oz sushi rice

2 tbsp rice vinegar

4 tsp caster sugar

½ tsp salt

2 sheets sushi nori

60 g/2½ oz smoked salmon

¼ cucumber, cut into fine strips

To serve:

wasabi

soy sauce

pickled ginger

TASTY TIP

If wasabi is unavailable, use a little horseradish. If unable to get sushi nori (seaweed sheets), shape the rice into small bite-size oblongs, then drape a piece of smoked salmon over each one and garnish with chives.

1 Rinse the rice thoroughly in cold water, until the water runs clear, then place in a pan with 300 ml/½ pint of water. Bring to the boil and cover with a tight-fitting lid. Reduce to a simmer and cook gently for 10 minutes. Turn the heat off, but keep the pan covered, to allow the rice to steam for a further 10 minutes.

2 In a small saucepan gently heat the rice vinegar, sugar and salt until the sugar has dissolved. When the rice has finished steaming, pour over the vinegar mixture and stir well to mix. Empty the rice out on to a large flat surface (a chopping board or large plate is ideal). Fan the rice to cool and to produce a shinier rice.

3 Lay one sheet of sushi nori on a sushi mat (if you do not have a sushi mat, improvise with a stiff piece of fabric that is a little larger than the sushi nori) and spread with half the cooled rice. Dampen the hands while doing this (this helps to prevent the rice from sticking to the hands). On the nearest edge place half the salmon and half the cucumber strips.

4 Roll up the rice and smoked salmon into a tight Swiss roll-like shape. Dampen the blade of a sharp knife and cut the sushi into slices about 2 cm/¾ inch thick. Repeat with the remaining sushi nori, rice, smoked salmon and cucumber. Serve with wasabi, soy sauce and pickled ginger.

2

3

4

Honey & Ginger Prawns

INGREDIENTS

Serves 4

1 carrot

50 g/2 oz bamboo shoots

4 spring onions

1 tbsp clear honey

1 tbsp tomato ketchup

1 tsp soy sauce

2.5 cm/1 inch piece fresh root ginger,
   peeled and finely grated

1 garlic clove, peeled and crushed

1 tbsp lime juice

175 g/6 oz peeled prawns, thawed
   if frozen

2 heads little gem lettuce leaves

2 tbsp freshly chopped coriander

salt and freshly ground black pepper

To garnish:

fresh coriander sprigs

lime slices

HELPFUL HINT

This highly versatile dish can be adapted to suit any diet. If liked, raw tiger prawns can be used for this recipe – do make sure if using raw prawns that the black vein that runs along their back is removed.

1 Cut the carrot into matchstick-size pieces, roughly chop the bamboo shoots and finely slice the spring onions.

2 Combine the bamboo shoots with the carrot matchsticks and spring onions.

3 In a wok or large frying pan gently heat the honey, tomato ketchup, soy sauce, ginger, garlic and lime juice with 3 tablespoons of water. Bring to the boil.

4 Add the carrot mixture and stir-fry for 2–3 minutes until the vegetables are hot.

5 Add the prawns and continue to stir-fry for 2 minutes.

6 Remove the wok or frying pan from the heat and reserve until cooled slightly.

7 Divide the little gem lettuce into leaves and rinse lightly.

8 Stir the chopped coriander into the prawn mixture and season to taste with salt and pepper. Spoon into the lettuce leaves and serve immediately garnished with sprigs of fresh coriander and lime slices.

1

5

8

Crostini with Chicken Livers

INGREDIENTS

Serves 4

2 tbsp olive oil
2 tbsp butter
1 shallot, peeled and finely chopped
1 garlic clove, peeled and crushed
150 g/5 oz chicken livers
1 tbsp plain flour
2 tbsp dry white wine
1 tbsp brandy
50 g/2 oz mushrooms, sliced
salt and freshly ground black pepper
4 slices of ciabatta or similar bread

To garnish:

fresh sage leaves
lemon wedges

TASTY TIP

If you prefer a lower-fat alternative to the fried bread in this recipe, omit 1 tablespoon of the butter and brush the bread slices with the remaining 1 tablespoon of oil. Bake in a preheated oven 180°C/350°F/Gas Mark 4 for about 20 minutes, or until golden and crisp then serve as above.

1 Heat 1 tablespoon of the olive oil and 1 tablespoon of the butter in a frying pan, add the shallot and garlic and cook gently for 2–3 minutes.

2 Trim and wash the chicken livers thoroughly and pat dry on absorbent kitchen paper. Cut into slices, then toss in the flour. Add the livers to the frying pan with the shallot and garlic and continue to fry for a further 2 minutes, stirring continuously.

3 Pour in the white wine and brandy and bring to the boil. Boil rapidly for 1–2 minutes to allow the alcohol to evaporate, then stir in the sliced mushrooms and cook gently for about 5 minutes, or until the chicken livers are cooked, but just a little pink inside. Season to taste with salt and pepper.

4 Fry the slices of ciabatta or similar-style bread in the remaining oil and butter, then place on individual serving dishes. Spoon over the liver mixture and garnish with a few sage leaves and lemon wedges. Serve immediately.

2

3

3

Mussels with Creamy Garlic & Saffron Sauce

INGREDIENTS

Serves 4

700 g/1½ lb fresh live mussels
300 ml/½ pint good quality dry
    white wine
1 tbsp olive oil
1 shallot, peeled and finely chopped
2 garlic cloves, peeled and crushed
1 tbsp freshly chopped oregano
2 saffron strands
150 ml/¼ pint single cream
salt and freshly ground black pepper
fresh crusty bread, to serve

HELPFUL HINT

Mussels are now farmed and are available most of the year. However, always try to buy mussels the day you intend to eat them. Place them in a bowl of cold water in the refrigerator as soon as possible, changing the water at least every 2 hours. If live mussels are unavailable, use prepacked, cooked mussels.

1 Clean the mussels thoroughly in plenty of cold water and remove any beards and barnacles from the shells. Discard any mussels that are open or damaged. Place in a large bowl and cover with cold water and leave in the refrigerator until required, if prepared earlier.

2 Pour the wine into a large saucepan and bring to the boil. Tip the mussels into the pan, cover and cook, shaking the saucepan periodically for 6–8 minutes, or until the mussels have opened completely.

3 Discard any mussels with closed shells, then using a slotted spoon, carefully remove the remaining open mussels from the saucepan and keep them warm. Reserve the cooking liquor.

4 Heat the olive oil in a small frying pan and cook the shallot and garlic gently for 2–3 minutes, until softened. Add the reserved cooking liquid and chopped oregano and cook for a further 3–4 minutes. Stir in the saffron and the cream and heat through gently. Season to taste with salt and pepper. Place a few mussels in individual serving bowls and spoon over the saffron sauce. Serve immediately with plenty of fresh crusty bread.

Hot Tiger Prawns with Parma Ham

INGREDIENTS

Serves 4

¹/₂ cucumber, peeled if preferred

4 ripe tomatoes

12 raw tiger prawns

6 tbsp olive oil

4 garlic cloves, peeled and crushed

4 tbsp freshly chopped parsley

salt and freshly ground black pepper

6 slices of Parma ham, cut in half

4 slices flat Italian bread

4 tbsp dry white wine

HELPFUL HINT

The black intestinal vein needs to be removed from raw prawns because it can cause a bitter flavour. Remove the shell, then using a small, sharp knife, make a cut along the centre back of the prawn and open out the flesh. Using the tip of the knife, remove the thread that lies along the length of the prawn and discard.

1 Preheat oven to 180°C/350°F/Gas Mark 4. Slice the cucumber and tomatoes thinly, then arrange on 4 large plates and reserve. Peel the prawns, leaving the tail shell intact and remove the thin black vein running down the back.

2 Whisk together 4 tablespoons of the olive oil, garlic and chopped parsley in a small bowl and season to taste with plenty of salt and pepper. Add the prawns to the mixture and stir until they are well coated. Remove the prawns, then wrap each one in a piece of Parma ham and secure with a cocktail stick.

3 Place the prepared prawns on a lightly oiled baking sheet or dish with the slices of bread and cook in the preheated oven for 5 minutes.

4 Remove the prawns from the oven and spoon the wine over the prawns and bread. Return to the oven and cook for a further 10 minutes until piping hot.

5 Carefully remove the cocktail sticks and arrange 3 prawn rolls on each slice of bread. Place on top of the sliced cucumber and tomatoes and serve immediately.

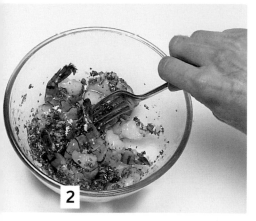
2

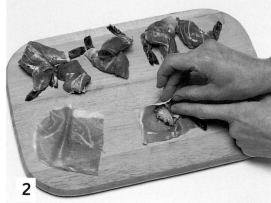
2

4

Mozzarella Parcels with Cranberry Relish

INGREDIENTS

Serves 6

125 g/4 oz mozzarella cheese
8 slices of thin white bread
2 medium eggs, beaten
salt and freshly ground black pepper
300 ml/½ pint olive oil

For the relish:
125 g/4 oz cranberries
2 tbsp fresh orange juice
grated rind of 1 small orange
50 g/2 oz soft light brown sugar
1 tbsp port

1 Slice the mozzarella thinly, remove the crusts from the bread and make sandwiches with the bread and cheese. Cut into 5 cm/2 inch squares and squash them quite flat. Season the eggs with salt and pepper, then soak the bread in the seasoned egg for 1 minute on each side until well coated.

2 Heat the oil to 190°C/375°F and deep-fry the bread squares for 1–2 minutes, or until they are crisp and golden brown. Drain on absorbent kitchen paper and keep warm while the cranberry relish is prepared.

3 Place the cranberries, orange juice, rind, sugar and port into a small saucepan and add 5 tablespoons of water. Bring to the boil, then simmer for 10 minutes, or until the cranberries have 'popped'. Sweeten with a little more sugar if necessary.

4 Arrange the mozzarella parcels on individual serving plates. Serve with a little of the cranberry relish.

HELPFUL HINT

To test the temperature of the oil without a thermometer, drop a cube of bread into the frying pan. If the bread browns in 30 seconds the oil is at the right temperature. If it does not, try again in a couple of minutes or increase the heat. If the bread goes very dark, reduce the temperature under the pan and add about 150 ml/¼ pint of cold oil and test again.

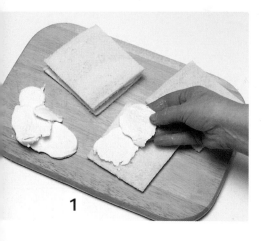
1

1

3

Fresh Tagliatelle with Courgettes

INGREDIENTS

Serves 4–6

225 g/8 oz strong plain bread flour
  or type oo pasta flour, plus extra
  for rolling
1 tsp salt
2 medium eggs
1 medium egg yolk
3 tbsp extra-virgin olive oil
2 small courgettes, halved
  lengthways and thinly sliced
2 garlic cloves, peeled and
  thinly sliced
large pinch chilli flakes
zest of ½ lemon
1 tbsp freshly shredded basil
salt and freshly ground black pepper
freshly grated Parmesan cheese,
  to serve

1 Sift the flour and salt into a large bowl, make a well in the centre and add the eggs and yolk, 1 tablespoon of oil with 1 teaspoon of water. Gradually mix to form a soft but not sticky dough, adding a little more flour or water as necessary. Turn out onto a lightly floured surface and knead for 5 minutes, or until smooth and elastic. Wrap in clingfilm and leave to rest at room temperature for about 30 minutes.

2 Divide the dough into 8 pieces. Feed a piece of dough through a pasta machine. Gradually decrease the settings on the rollers, feeding the pasta through each time, until the sheet is very long and thin. If the pasta seems sticky, dust the work surface and both sides of the pasta generously with flour. Cut in half crosswise and hang over a clean pole. Repeat with the remaining dough. Leave to dry for about 5 minutes. Feed each sheet through the tagliatelle cutter, hanging the cut pasta over the pole. Leave to dry for a further 5 minutes. Wind a handful of pasta strands into nests and leave on a floured tea towel. Repeat with the remaining dough and leave to dry for 5 minutes.

3 Cook the pasta in plenty of salted boiling water for 2–3 minutes, or until 'al dente'.

4 Meanwhile, heat the remaining oil in a large frying pan and add the courgettes, garlic, chilli and lemon zest. Cook over a medium heat for 3–4 minutes, or until the courgettes are lightly golden and tender.

5 Drain the pasta thoroughly, reserving 2 tablespoons of the cooking water. Add the pasta to the courgettes with the basil and seasoning. Mix well, adding the reserved cooking water. Serve with the Parmesan cheese.

1

2

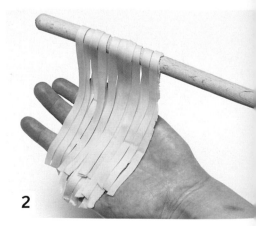

2

Beetroot Ravioli with Dill Cream Sauce

INGREDIENTS

Serves 4–6

fresh pasta (see Fresh Tagliatelle
   with Courgettes, page 46)
1 tbsp olive oil
1 small onion, peeled and
   finely chopped
½ tsp caraway seeds
175 g/6 oz cooked beetroot, chopped
175 g/6 oz ricotta cheese
25 g/1 oz fresh white breadcrumbs
1 medium egg yolk
2 tbsp grated Parmesan cheese
salt and freshly ground black pepper
4 tbsp walnut oil
4 tbsp freshly chopped dill
1 tbsp green peppercorns, drained
   and roughly chopped
6 tbsp crème fraîche

1. Make the pasta dough according to the recipe on page 46. Wrap in clingfilm and leave to rest for 30 minutes.

2. Heat the olive oil in a large frying pan, add the onion and caraway seeds and cook over a medium heat for 5 minutes, or until the onion is softened and lightly golden. Stir in the beetroot and cook for 5 minutes.

3. Blend the beetroot mixture in a food processor until smooth, then allow to cool. Stir in the ricotta cheese, breadcrumbs, egg yolk and Parmesan cheese. Season the filling to taste with salt and pepper and reserve.

4. Divide the pasta dough into 8 pieces. Roll out as for tagliatelle, but do not cut the sheets in half. Lay 1 sheet on a floured surface and place 5 heaped teaspoons of the filling 2.5 cm/1 inch apart.

5. Dampen around the heaps of filling and lay a second sheet of pasta over the top. Press around the heaps to seal.

6. Cut into squares using a pastry wheel or sharp knife. Put the filled pasta shapes onto a floured tea towel.

7. Bring a large pan of lightly salted water to a rolling boil. Drop the ravioli into the boiling water, return to the boil and cook for 3–4 minutes, until 'al dente'.

8. Meanwhile, heat the walnut oil in a small pan then add the chopped dill and green peppercorns. Remove from the heat, stir in the crème fraîche and season well. Drain the cooked pasta thoroughly and toss with the sauce. Tip into warmed serving dishes and serve immediately.

4

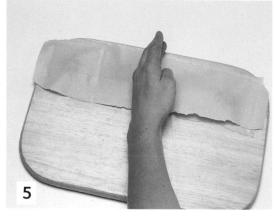

5

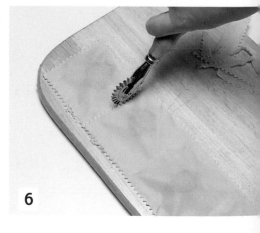

6

Tagliatelle with Brown Butter, Asparagus & Parmesan

INGREDIENTS

Serves 6

fresh pasta (see Fresh Tagliatelle with
   Courgettes, page 46) or 450 g/1 lb
   dried tagliatelle, such as the white
   and green variety

350 g/12 oz asparagus, trimmed and
   cut into short lengths

75 g/3 oz unsalted butter

1 garlic clove, peeled and sliced

25 g/1 oz flaked hazelnuts or whole
   hazelnuts, roughly chopped

1 tbsp freshly chopped parsley

1 tbsp freshly snipped chives

salt and freshly ground black pepper

50 g/2 oz freshly grated Parmesan
   cheese, to serve

FOOD FACT

Asparagus is available all year round, but is at its best during May and June. If you buy loose asparagus, rather than pre-packed, choose stems of similar thickness so they will all cook in the same time.

1   If using fresh pasta, prepare the dough according to the recipe on page 46. Cut into tagliatelle, wind into nests and reserve on a floured tea towel until ready to cook.

2   Bring a pan of lightly salted water to the boil. Add the asparagus and cook for 1 minute. Drain immediately, refresh under cold running water and drain again. Pat dry and reserve.

3   Melt the butter in a large frying pan, then add the garlic and hazelnuts and cook over a medium heat until the butter turns golden. Immediately remove from the heat and add the parsley, chives and asparagus. Leave for 2–3 minutes, until the asparagus is heated through.

4   Meanwhile, bring a large pan of lightly salted water to a rolling boil, then add the pasta nests. Cook until 'al dente': 2–3 minutes for fresh pasta and according to the packet instructions for dried pasta. Drain the pasta thoroughly and return to the pan. Add the asparagus mixture and toss together. Season to taste with salt and pepper and tip into a warmed serving dish. Serve immediately with grated Parmesan cheese.

2

3

4

Louisiana Prawns & Fettuccine

INGREDIENTS

Serves 4

4 tbsp olive oil

450 g/1 lb raw tiger prawns, washed
   and peeled, shells and
   heads reserved

2 shallots, peeled and finely chopped

4 garlic cloves, peeled and
   finely chopped

large handful fresh basil leaves

1 carrot, peeled and finely chopped

1 onion, peeled and finely chopped

1 celery stick, trimmed and
   finely chopped

2–3 sprigs fresh parsley

2–3 sprigs fresh thyme

salt and freshly ground black pepper

pinch cayenne pepper

175 ml/6 fl oz dry white wine

450 g/1 lb ripe tomatoes,
   roughly chopped

juice of ½ lemon, or to taste

350 g/12 oz fettuccine

1. Heat 2 tablespoons of the olive oil in a large saucepan and add the reserved prawn shells and heads. Fry over a high heat for 2–3 minutes, until the shells turn pink and are lightly browned. Add half the shallots, half the garlic, half the basil and the carrot, onion, celery, parsley and thyme. Season lightly with salt, pepper and cayenne and sauté for 2–3 minutes, stirring often.

2. Pour in the wine and stir, scraping the pan well. Bring to the boil and simmer for 1 minute, then add the tomatoes. Cook for a further 3–4 minutes then pour in 200 ml/7 fl oz water. Bring to the boil, lower the heat and simmer for about 30 minutes, stirring often and using a wooden spoon to mash the prawn shells in order to release as much flavour as possible into the sauce. Lower the heat if the sauce is reducing very quickly.

3. Strain through a sieve, pressing well to extract as much liquid as possible; there should be about 450 ml/¾ pint. Pour the liquid into a clean pan and bring to the boil, then lower the heat and simmer gently until the liquid is reduced by about half.

4. Heat the remaining olive oil over a high heat in a clean frying pan and add the peeled prawns. Season lightly and add the lemon juice. Cook for 1 minute, lower the heat and add the remaining shallots and garlic. Cook for 1 minute. Add the sauce and adjust the seasoning.

5. Meanwhile, bring a large pan of lightly salted water to a rolling boil and add the fettuccine. Cook according to the packet instructions, or until 'al dente', and drain thoroughly. Transfer to a warmed serving dish. Add the sauce and toss well. Garnish with the remaining basil and serve immediately.

1

2

3

Pasta with Walnut Sauce

INGREDIENTS

Serves 4

50 g/2 oz walnuts, toasted
3 spring onions, trimmed
  and chopped
2 garlic cloves, peeled and sliced
1 tbsp freshly chopped parsley
  or basil
5 tbsp extra-virgin olive oil
salt and freshly ground black pepper
450 g/1 lb broccoli, cut into florets
350 g/12 oz pasta shapes
1 red chilli, deseeded and
  finely chopped

HELPFUL HINT

There is no hard-and-fast rule about which shape of pasta to use with this recipe; it is really a matter of personal preference. Spirali have been used here, but rigatoni, farfalle, garganelle or pipe rigate would all work well, or you could choose flavoured pasta, such as tomato, or a wholewheat variety for a change.

1 Place the toasted walnuts in a blender or food processor with the chopped spring onions, one of the garlic cloves and parsley or basil. Blend to a fairly smooth paste, then gradually add 3 tablespoons of the olive oil, until it is well mixed into the paste. Season the walnut paste to taste with salt and pepper and reserve.

2 Bring a large pan of lightly salted water to a rolling boil. Add the broccoli, return to the boil and cook for 2 minutes. Remove the broccoli, using a slotted draining spoon and refresh under cold running water. Drain again and pat dry on absorbent kitchen paper.

3 Bring the water back to a rolling boil. Add the pasta and cook according to the packet instructions, or until 'al dente'.

4 Meanwhile, heat the remaining oil in a frying pan. Add the remaining garlic and chilli. Cook gently for 2 minutes, or until softened. Add the broccoli and walnut paste. Cook for a further 3–4 minutes, or until heated through.

5 Drain the pasta thoroughly and transfer to a large warmed serving bowl. Pour over the walnut and broccoli sauce. Toss together, adjust the seasoning and serve immediately.

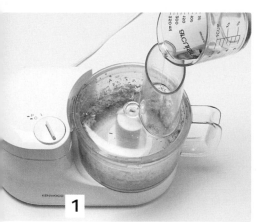

Linguine with Fennel, Crab & Chervil

INGREDIENTS

Serves 6

450g/1 lb linguine
25 g/1 oz butter
2 carrots, peeled and finely diced
2 shallots, peeled and finely diced
2 celery sticks, trimmed and
   finely diced
1 bulb fennel, trimmed and
   finely diced
6 spring onions, trimmed and
   finely chopped
300 ml/½ pint double cream
3 tbsp freshly chopped chervil
1 large cooked crab,
   plus extra for garnish
salt and freshly ground pepper
juice of ½ lemon, or to taste
sprig of dill, to garnish

HELPFUL HINT

When cooking pasta, use a very large saucepan so that the pasta has plenty of space to move around freely. Once the water has come to the boil, add the pasta, stir, cover and return to the boil. The lid can then be removed so that the water does not boil over.

1   Bring a large pan of lightly salted water to a rolling boil. Add the pasta and cook according to the packet instructions, or until 'al dente'.

2   Meanwhile, heat the butter in a large saucepan. Add the carrots, shallots, celery, fennel and three-quarters of the chopped spring onions. Cook the vegetables gently for 8–10 minutes, or until tender, stirring frequently and ensuring that they do not brown.

3   Add the double cream and chopped chervil to the vegetable mixture. Scrape the crab meat over the sauce, then stir to mix the sauce ingredients.

4   Season the sauce to taste with salt and pepper and stir in the lemon juice. Drain the pasta thoroughly and transfer to a large warmed serving dish. Pour over the sauce and toss. Garnish with extra chervil, the remaining spring onions and a sprig of dill. Serve immediately.

Poached Fish Dumplings with Creamy Chilli Sauce

INGREDIENTS

Serves 4

450 g/1 lb white fish fillet, skinned
  and boned
1 tsp dark soy sauce
1 tbsp cornflour
1 medium egg yolk
salt and freshly ground black pepper
3 tbsp freshly chopped coriander,
  plus extra, to garnish
1.6 litres/2¾ pints fish stock

For the creamy chilli sauce:

2 tsp groundnut oil
2 garlic cloves, peeled and
  finely chopped
4 spring onions, trimmed and
  finely sliced
2 tbsp dry sherry
1 tbsp sweet chilli sauce
1 tbsp light soy sauce
1 tbsp lemon juice
6 tbsp crème fraîche

To garnish:

sprigs of fresh coriander
fresh carrot sticks

1. Chop the fish into chunks and place in a food processor with the soy sauce, cornflour and egg yolk. Season to taste with salt and pepper. Blend until fairly smooth. Add the coriander and process for a few seconds until well mixed. Transfer to a bowl, cover and chill in the refrigerator for 30 minutes.

2. With damp hands shape the chilled mixture into walnut-sized balls and place on a baking tray lined with non-stick baking paper. Chill in the refrigerator for a further 30 minutes.

3. Pour the stock into a wide saucepan, bring to the boil, then reduce the heat until barely simmering. Add the fish balls and poach for 3–4 minutes or until cooked through.

4. Meanwhile, make the sauce. Heat the oil in a small saucepan, add the garlic and spring onions and cook until golden. Stir in the sherry, chilli and soy sauces and lemon juice, then remove immediately from the heat. Stir in the crème fraîche and season to taste with salt and pepper.

5. Using a slotted spoon, lift the cooked fish balls from the stock and place on a warmed serving dish. Drizzle over the sauce, garnish with sprigs of fresh coriander and serve immediately.

1

2

3

Smoked Mackerel Vol-au-Vents

INGREDIENTS

Makes 12

350 g/12 oz prepared puff pastry
1 small egg, beaten
2 tsp sesame seeds
225 g/8 oz peppered smoked
  mackerel, skinned and chopped
5 cm/2 inch piece cucumber
4 tbsp soft cream cheese
2 tbsp cranberry sauce
1 tbsp freshly chopped dill
1 tbsp finely grated lemon rind
dill sprigs, to garnish
mixed salad leaves, to serve

FOOD FACT

Mackerel is a relatively cheap fish and one of the richest sources of minerals, oils and vitamins available. This dish is an affordable way to incorporate all these essential nutrients into your diet.

1 Preheat the oven to 230°C/450°F/Gas Mark 8. Roll the pastry out on a lightly floured surface and using a 9 cm/3½ inch fluted cutter cut out 12 rounds.

2 Using a 1 cm/½ inch cutter mark a lid in the centre of each round.

3 Place on a damp baking sheet and brush the rounds with a little beaten egg.

4 Sprinkle the pastry with the sesame seeds and bake in the preheated oven for 10–12 minutes, or until golden brown and well risen.

5 Transfer the vol-au-vents to a chopping board and, when cool enough to touch, carefully remove the lids with a small sharp knife.

6 Scoop out any uncooked pastry from the inside of each vol-au-vent, then return to the oven for 5–8 minutes to dry out. Remove and allow to cool.

7 Flake the mackerel into small pieces and reserve. Peel the cucumber if desired, cut into very small dice and add to the mackerel.

8 Beat the soft cream cheese with the cranberry sauce, dill and lemon rind. Stir in the mackerel and cucumber and use to fill the vol-au-vents. Place the lids on top and garnish dill sprigs.

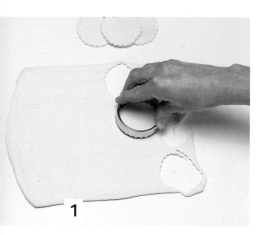

1

5

8

Garlic Wild Mushroom Galettes

INGREDIENTS

Serves 6

1 quantity quick flaky pastry
  (see page 66), chilled
1 onion, peeled
1 red chilli, deseeded
2 garlic cloves, peeled
275 g/10 oz mixed mushrooms,
  e.g. oysters, chestnuts, morels,
  ceps and chanterelles
25 g/1 oz butter
2 tbsp freshly chopped parsley
125 g/4 oz mozzarella cheese, sliced

To serve:
cherry tomatoes
mixed green salad leaves

HELPFUL HINT

Many supermarkets now stock a variety of wild mushrooms, all of which can be used in this recipe. It is important to maintain as much of the flavour of the mushrooms as possible, so do not peel mushrooms unless they appear old or tough. Either rinse lightly if covered with small pieces of soil or wipe well, trim the stalks and use.

1 Preheat the oven to 220°C/425°F/Gas Mark 7. On a lightly floured surface roll out the chilled pastry very thinly.

2 Cut out 6 x 15 cm/6 inch circles and place on a lightly oiled baking sheet.

3 Thinly slice the onion, then divide into rings and reserve.

4 Thinly slice the chilli and slice the garlic into wafer-thin slivers. Add to the onions and reserve.

5 Wipe or lightly rinse the mushrooms. Halve or quarter any large mushrooms and keep the small ones whole.

6 Heat the butter in a frying pan and sauté the onion, chilli and garlic gently for about 3 minutes. Add the mushrooms and cook for about 5 minutes, or until beginning to soften.

7 Stir the parsley into the mushroom mixture and drain off any excess liquid.

8 Pile the mushroom mixture on to the pastry circles within 5 mm/ $\frac{1}{4}$ inches of the edge. Arrange the sliced mozzarella cheese on top.

9 Bake in the preheated oven for 12–15 minutes, or until golden brown and serve with the tomatoes and salad.

2

5

8

French Onion Tart

INGREDIENTS

Serves 4

For the quick, flaky pastry:
125 g/4 oz butter
175 g/6 oz plain flour
pinch of salt

For the filling:
2 tbsp olive oil
4 large onions, peeled and
  thinly sliced
3 tbsp white wine vinegar
2 tbsp muscovado sugar
a little beaten egg or milk
175 g/6 oz Cheddar
  cheese, grated
salt and freshly ground
  black pepper

1 Preheat the oven to 200°C/400°F/Gas Mark 6. Place the butter in the freezer for 30 minutes. Sift the flour and salt into a large bowl. Remove the butter from the freezer and grate using the coarse side of a grater, dipping the butter in the flour every now and again as it makes it easier to grate.

2 Mix the butter into the flour, using a knife, making sure all the butter is coated thoroughly with flour.

3 Add 2 tablespoons of cold water and continue to mix, bringing the mixture together. Use your hands to complete the mixing. Add a little more water if needed to leave a clean bowl. Place the pastry in a polythene bag and chill in the refrigerator for 30 minutes.

4 Heat the oil in a large frying pan, then fry the onions for 10 minutes, stirring occasionally until softened.

5 Stir in the white wine vinegar and sugar. Increase the heat and stir frequently, for another 4–5 minutes until the onions turn a deep caramel colour. Cook for another 5 minutes, then reserve to cool.

6 On a lightly floured surface, roll out the pastry to a 35.5 cm/14 inch circle. Wrap over a rolling pin and move the circle onto a baking sheet.

7 Sprinkle half the cheese over the pastry, leaving a 5 cm/2 inch border around the edge, then spoon the caramelised onions over the cheese.

8 Fold the uncovered pastry edges over the edge of the filling to form a rim and brush the rim with beaten egg or milk.

9 Season to taste, sprinkle over the remaining Cheddar and bake for 20–25 minutes. Transfer to a large plate and serve immediately.

1

4

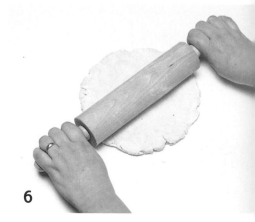
6

Olive & Feta Parcels

INGREDIENTS

Makes 30

1 small red pepper
1 small yellow pepper
125 g/4 oz assorted marinated green
  and black olives
125 g/4 oz feta cheese
2 tbsp pine nuts, lightly toasted
6 sheets filo pastry
3 tbsp olive oil
sour cream and chive dip, to serve

HELPFUL HINT

Feta is generally made from goats' milk and has quite a salty taste. To make the cheese less salty simply soak it in milk, then drain before eating.

1   Preheat the oven to 180°C/350°F/Gas Mark 4. Preheat the grill, then line the grill rack with tinfoil.

2   Cut the peppers into quarters and remove the seeds. Place skin-side up on the foil-lined grill rack and cook under the preheated grill for 10 minutes, turning occasionally until the skins begin to blacken.

3   Place the peppers in a polythene bag and leave until cool enough to handle, then skin and thinly slice.

4   Chop the olives and cut the feta cheese into small cubes. Mix together the olives, feta, sliced peppers and pine nuts.

5   Cut 1 sheet of filo pastry in half then brush with a little of the oil. Place a spoonful of the olive and feta mix about one-third of the way up the pastry.

6   Fold over the pastry and wrap to form a square parcel encasing the filling completely.

7   Place this parcel in the centre of the second half of the pastry sheet. Brush the edges lightly with a little oil, bring up the corners to meet in the centre and twist them loosely to form a purse.

8   Brush with a little more oil and repeat with the remaining filo pastry and filling.

9   Place the parcels on a lightly oiled baking sheet and bake in the preheated oven for 10–15 minutes, or until crisp and golden brown. Serve with the dip.

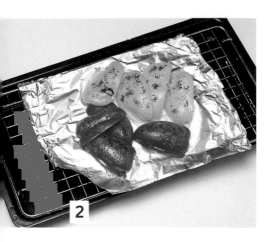

2

5

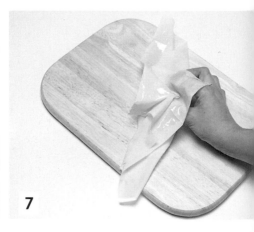

7

Fettuccine with Wild Mushrooms & Prosciutto

INGREDIENTS

Serves 6

15 g/½ oz dried porcini mushrooms
150 ml/¼ pint hot chicken stock
2 tbsp olive oil
1 small onion, peeled and
  finely chopped
2 garlic cloves, peeled and
  finely chopped
4 slices prosciutto, chopped or torn
225 g/8 oz mixed wild or cultivated
  mushrooms, wiped and sliced
  if necessary
450 g/1 lb fettuccine
3 tbsp crème fraîche
2 tbsp freshly chopped parsley
salt and freshly ground black pepper
freshly grated Parmesan cheese,
  to serve (optional)

FOOD FACT

Prosciutto is produced from pigs fed on whey. The ham is dry cured, then weighted to flatten it and give it a dense texture. The delicious flavour develops during the year it is allowed to mature.

1 Place the dried mushrooms in a small bowl and pour over the hot chicken stock. Leave to soak for 15–20 minutes, or until the mushrooms have softened.

2 Meanwhile, heat the olive oil in a large frying pan. Add the onion and cook for 5 minutes over a medium heat, or until softened. Add the garlic and cook for 1 minute, then add the prosciutto and cook for a further minute.

3 Drain the dried mushrooms, reserving the soaking liquid. Roughly chop and add to the frying pan together with the fresh mushrooms. Cook over a high heat for 5 minutes, stirring often, or until softened. Strain the mushroom soaking liquid into the pan.

4 Meanwhile, bring a large pan of lightly salted water to a rolling boil. Add the pasta and cook according to the packet instructions, or until 'al dente'.

5 Stir the crème fraîche and chopped parsley into the mushroom mixture and heat through gently. Season to taste with salt and pepper. Drain the pasta well, transfer to a large warmed serving dish and pour over the sauce. Serve immediately with grated Parmesan cheese.

1

2

3

Prunes Stuffed with Mussels

INGREDIENTS

Serves 6

3 tbsp port
1 tbsp clear honey
2 cloves garlic, crushed
24 large stoned prunes
24 live mussels
12 rashers smoked streaky bacon
salt and pepper

1 Mix together the port, honey and garlic then season. Put the prunes into a small bowl and pour over the port mixture. Cover and leave to marinate for at least 4 hours and preferably overnight.

2 Next day, clean the mussels by scrubbing or scraping the shells and pulling out any beards. Put the mussels in a large saucepan with just the water that clings to their shells. Cook, covered, over a high heat for 3–4 minutes until all the mussels have opened. Discard any mussels that remain closed.

3 Drain the mussels, reserving the cooking liquid. Allow to cool then remove the mussels from their shells.

4 Using the back of a knife, stretch the bacon rashers then cut in half widthways. Lift the prunes from their marinade, reserving any that remains.

5 Stuff each prune with a mussel then wrap with a piece of bacon. Secure with a cocktail stick. Repeat to make 24.

6 In a saucepan, simmer together the mussel cooking liquid and remaining marinade until reduced and syrupy. Brush the stuffed prunes with this mixture. Place under a preheated hot grill and cook for 3–4 minutes each side, turning regularly and brushing with the marinade, until the bacon is crisp and golden. Serve while still hot.

3

4

5

Stuffed Squid

INGREDIENTS

Serves 4

12 baby squid, cleaned
1 tsp salt
4 tbsp olive oil
1 small onion, finely chopped
1 garlic clove, finely chopped
40g /1³/₄ oz basmati rice
1 tbsp seedless raisins
1 tbsp pine nuts, toasted
1 tbsp fresh flat-leaf parsley, chopped
400 g/14 oz can chopped tomatoes
25 g/1 oz sun-dried tomatoes in oil,
   drained and finely chopped
120 ml/4 fl oz dry white wine
salt and pepper
crusty bread, to serve

1 Separate the tentacles from the body of the squid. Chop the tentacles and set aside. Rub the squid tubes inside and out with the salt and set aside while you prepare the stuffing.

2 Heat 1 tablespoon of the olive oil in a frying pan and add the onion and garlic. Cook for 4–5 minutes until softened and lightly browned. Add the chopped tentacles and fry for 2–3 minutes. Add the rice, raisins, pine nuts, parsley and seasoning. Remove from the heat.

3 Allow the rice mixture to cool slightly and spoon it into the squid tubes, about three quarters full to allow the rice to expand. You may need to open the squid tubes a little by making a small cut. Secure each filled squid with a cocktail stick.

4 Heat the remaining oil in a large flameproof casserole dish. Add the squid and fry for a few minutes on all sides until lightly browned. Add the tomatoes, sun-dried tomatoes, wine and seasoning. Bake in a preheated oven at 180°C/350°F/Gas Mark 4, for 45 minutes. Serve hot or cold with plenty of crusty bread.

TASTY TIP

If you have difficulty finding baby squid, larger ones work very well and the cooking time is the same. Use cleaned squid weighing 8 oz in total for the amount of stuffing in this recipe.

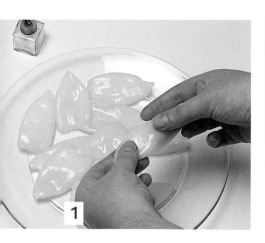

1

2

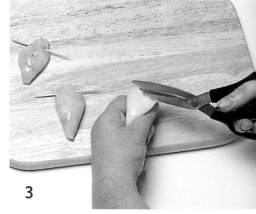

3

Dim Sum Pork Parcels

INGREDIENTS

Makes about 40

125 g/4 oz canned water chestnuts, drained and finely chopped
125 g/4 oz raw prawns, peeled, deveined and coarsely chopped
350 g/12 oz fresh pork mince
2 tbsp smoked bacon, finely chopped
1 tbsp light soy sauce, plus extra, to serve
1 tsp dark soy sauce
1 tbsp Chinese rice wine
2 tbsp fresh root ginger, peeled and finely chopped
3 spring onions, trimmed and finely chopped
2 tsp sesame oil
1 medium egg white, lightly beaten
salt and freshly ground black pepper
2 tsp sugar
40 wonton skins, thawed if frozen
toasted sesame seeds, to garnish
soy sauce, to serve

FOOD FACT

These steamed dumplings are known as shao mai in China, meaning 'cook and sell' and are a popular street food.

1 Place the water chestnuts, prawns, pork mince and bacon in a bowl and mix together. Add the soy sauces, Chinese rice wine, ginger, chopped spring onion, sesame oil and egg white. Season to taste with salt and pepper, sprinkle in the sugar and mix the filling thoroughly.

2 Place a spoonful of filling in the centre of a wonton skin. Bring the sides up and press around the filling to make a basket shape. Flatten the base of the skin, so the wonton stands solid. The top should be wide open, exposing the filling.

3 Place the parcels on a heatproof plate, on a wire rack inside a wok or on the base of a muslin-lined bamboo steamer. Place over a wok, half-filled with boiling water, cover, then steam the parcels for about 20 minutes. Do this in 2 batches. Transfer to a warmed serving plate, sprinkle with toasted sesame seeds, drizzle with soy sauce and serve immediately.

1

2

3

Vitello Tonnato

INGREDIENTS

Serves 6

1 boned and rolled piece of veal leg, about 900 g/2 lb boned weight
olive oil
salt and pepper

For the tuna mayonnaise:

150 g/5½ oz can tuna in olive oil
2 large eggs
3 tbsp lemon juice
olive oil

To garnish:

8 black olives, stoned and halved
1 tbsp capers in brine, rinsed and drained
fresh flat-leaf parsley, finely chopped
lemon wedges

1 Rub the veal all over with oil and pepper and place in a roasting tin. Cover the meat with a piece of foil if there is not any fat on it, then roast in a preheated oven at 230°C/450°F/Gas Mark 8 for 10 minutes. Lower the heat to 180°C/350°F/Gas Mark 4 and continue roasting for 1 hour for medium, or 1¼ hours for well-done. Set the veal aside and leave to cool completely, reserving any juices in the roasting tin.

2 Meanwhile, drain the tuna, reserving the oil. Blend the eggs in a food processor with 1 teaspoon of the lemon juice and a pinch of salt. Add enough olive oil to the tuna oil to make up to 300 ml/10 fl oz.

3 With the motor running, add the oil to the eggs, drop by drop, until a thin mayonnaise forms. Add the tuna and process until smooth. Blend in the lemon juice to taste. Adjust the seasoning.

4 Slice the cool meat very thinly. Add any juices to the reserved pan juices. Gradually pour the veal juices into the tuna mayonnaise, whisking until a thin, pouring consistency.

5 Layer the veal slices with the sauce on a platter, ending with a layer of sauce. Cover and leave to chill overnight. Garnish with olives, capers and a light sprinkling of parsley. Arrange lemon wedges around the edge and serve.

3

4

5

Noisettes of Salmon

INGREDIENTS

Serves 4

4 salmon steaks
50 g/1 3/4 oz butter, softened
1 garlic clove, crushed
2 tsp mustard seeds
2 tbsp fresh thyme, chopped
1 tbsp fresh parsley, chopped
2 tbsp vegetable oil
4 tomatoes, skinned, deseeded
  and chopped
salt and pepper

To serve:
new potatoes
green vegetables or salad

1 Carefully remove the central bone from the salmon steaks and cut them in half. Curl each piece around to form a medallion and tie with string. Blend together the butter, garlic, mustard seeds, thyme, parsley and seasoning and set aside.

2 Heat the oil in a ridged pan or frying pan and brown the salmon noisettes on both sides, in batches if necessary. Drain on paper towels and leave to cool.

3 Cut 4 pieces of baking parchment into 30 cm/12 inch squares. Place 2 salmon noisettes on top of each square and top with a little of the flavoured butter and tomato. Draw up the edges of the paper and fold together to enclose the fish. Place on a baking sheet.

4 Cook in a preheated oven at 200°C/400°F/Gas Mark 6 for 10–15 minutes or until the salmon is cooked through. Serve immediately while still warm with new potatoes and a green vegetable of your choice.

HELPFUL HINT
You can make cod steaks into noisettes in the same way. Cook them with butter flavoured with chives and basil.

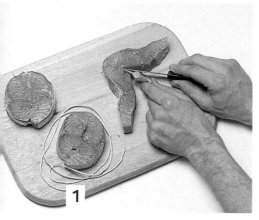

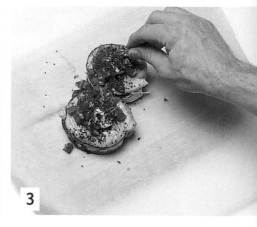

Stuffed Monkfish Tail

INGREDIENTS

Serves 4

750 g/1 lb 10 oz monkfish tail,
   skinned and trimmed
6 slices Parma ham
4 tbsp chopped mixed herbs such as
   parsley, chives, basil, sage
1 tsp finely grated lemon rind
2 tbsp olive oil
salt and pepper

To serve:
shredded stir-fried vegetables
new potatoes

1 Using a sharp knife, carefully cut down each side of the central bone of the monkfish to leave 2 fillets. Wash and dry the fillets.

2 Lay the Parma ham slices widthways on a clean work surface so that they overlap slightly. Lay the fish fillets lengthways on top of the ham so that the two cut sides face each other.

3 Mix together the chopped herbs and lemon rind. Season well. Pack this mixture on to the cut surface of one monkfish fillet. Press the 2 fillets together and wrap tightly with the Parma ham slices. Secure with string or cocktail sticks.

4 Heat the olive oil in a large ovenproof frying pan and place the fish in the pan, seam-side down first, and brown the wrapped monkfish tail all over.

5 Cook in a preheated oven, at 200°C/400°F/Gas Mark 6, for 25 minutes until golden and the fish is tender. Remove from the oven and allow to rest for 10 minutes before slicing thickly. Serve with shredded stir-fried vegetables and new potatoes.

TASTY TIP

It is possible to remove the central bone from a monkfish tail without separating the two fillets completely. This makes it easier to stuff, but takes some practice.

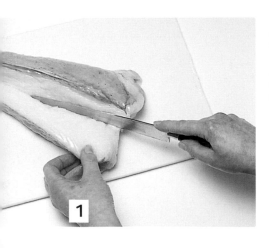

1

2

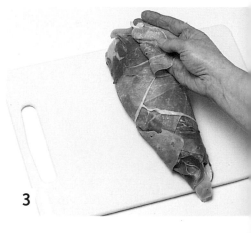

3

Parmesan & Garlic Lobster

INGREDIENTS

Serves 2

1 large cooked lobster
25 g/1 oz unsalted butter
4 garlic cloves, peeled and crushed
1 tbsp plain flour
300 ml/½ pint milk
125 g/4 oz Parmesan cheese, grated
sea salt and freshly ground
  black pepper
assorted salad leaves, to serve

1 Preheat oven to 180°C/350°F/Gas Mark 4, 10 minutes before cooking. Halve the lobster and crack the claws. Remove the gills, green sac behind the head and the black vein running down the body. Place the 2 lobster halves in a shallow ovenproof dish.

2 Melt the butter in a small saucepan and gently cook the garlic for 3 minutes, until softened. Add the flour and stir over a medium heat for 1 minute. Draw the saucepan off the heat then gradually stir in the milk, stirring until the sauce thickens. Return to the heat and cook for 2 minutes, stirring throughout until smooth and thickened. Stir in half the cheese and continue to cook for 1 minute, then season to taste with salt and pepper.

3 Pour the cheese sauce over the lobster halves and sprinkle with the remaining Parmesan cheese. Bake in the preheated oven for 20 minutes, or until heated through and the cheese sauce is golden brown. Serve with assorted salad leaves.

FOOD FACT

Nowadays we consider lobster to be a luxury, however, up until the end of 19th century lobster was so plentiful that it was used as fish bait.

HELPFUL HINT

This impressive-looking dish makes a wonderful meal for two. Make the sauce in advance and cover the surface with a layer of clingfilm. Refrigerate until ready to serve.

1

2

3

Seared Pancetta–wrapped Cod

INGREDIENTS

Serves 4

4 x 175 g/6 oz thick cod fillets
4 very thin slices of pancetta
3 tbsp capers in vinegar
1 tbsp of vegetable or sunflower oil
2 tbsp lemon juice
1 tbsp olive oil
freshly ground black pepper
1 tbsp freshly chopped parsley,
   to garnish

To serve:

freshly cooked vegetables
new potatoes

FOOD FACT

Pancetta is Italian-cured belly pork, which is often delicately smoked and sold either finely sliced or chopped roughly into small cubes. The slices of pancetta can be used to encase poultry and fish, whereas chopped pancetta is often used in sauces. To cook chopped pancetta, fry for 2–3 minutes and reserve. Use the oil to seal meat or to fry onions, then return the pancetta to the pan.

1 Wipe the cod fillets and wrap each one with the pancetta. Secure each fillet with a cocktail stick and reserve.

2 Drain the capers and soak in cold water for 10 minutes to remove any excess salt, then drain and reserve.

3 Heat the oil in a large frying pan and sear the wrapped pieces of cod fillet for about 3 minutes on each side, turning carefully with a fish slice so as not to break up the fish.

4 Lower the heat then continue to cook for 2–3 minutes or until the fish is cooked thoroughly.

5 Meanwhile, place the reserved capers, lemon juice and olive oil into a small saucepan. Grind over the black pepper.

6 Place the saucepan over a low heat and bring to a gentle simmer, stirring continuously for 2–3 minutes.

7 Once the fish is cooked, garnish with the parsley and serve with the warm caper dressing, freshly cooked vegetables and new potatoes.

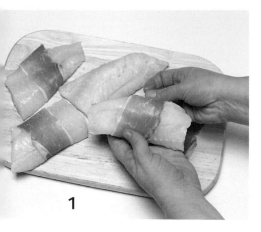

1

3

6

Mussels Linguine

INGREDIENTS

Serves 4

2 kg/4¹/₂ lb fresh mussels, washed
   and scrubbed
knob of butter
1 onion, peeled and finely chopped
300 ml/¹/₂ pint medium dry
   white wine

For the sauce:

1 tbsp sunflower oil
4 baby onions, peeled and quartered
2 garlic cloves, peeled and crushed
400 g can chopped tomatoes
large pinch of salt
225 g/8 oz dried linguine
   or tagliatelle
2 tbsp freshly chopped parsley

1. Soak the mussels in plenty of cold water. Leave in the refrigerator until required. When ready to use, scrub the mussel shells, removing any barnacles or beards. Discard any open mussels.

2. Melt the butter in a large pan. Add the mussels, onion and wine. Cover with a close-fitting lid and steam for 5–6 minutes, shaking the pan gently to ensure even cooking. Discard any mussels that have not opened, then strain and reserve the liquor.

3. To make the sauce, heat the oil in a medium-sized saucepan, and gently fry the quartered onion and garlic for 3–4 minutes until soft and transparent. Stir in the tomatoes and half the reserved mussel liquor. Bring to the boil and simmer for 7–10 minutes until the sauce begins to thicken.

4. Cook the pasta in boiling salted water for 7 minutes or or until 'al dente'. Drain the pasta, reserving 2 tablespoons of the cooking liquor, then return the pasta and liquor to the pan.

5. Remove the meat from half the mussel shells. Stir into the sauce along with the remaining mussels. Pour the hot sauce over the cooked pasta and toss gently. Garnish with the parsley and serve immediately.

TASTY TIP

Serving mussels in their shells is a fantastic way to eat them. Every mussel is surrounded with the delicious sauce, adding flavour to every mouthful. Clams, which often have a sweeter flavour, could also be used in this recipe.

1

2

5

Cod with Fennel & Cardamom

INGREDIENTS

Serves 4

1 garlic clove, peeled and crushed
finely grated rind of 1 lemon
1 tsp lemon juice
1 tbsp olive oil
1 fennel bulb
1 tbsp cardamom pods
salt and freshly ground black pepper
4 x 175 g/6 oz thick cod fillets

FOOD FACT

When buying fresh fish, look for fish that does not smell. Any ammonia-type smelling fish should be avoided. The flesh should be plump and firm-looking. The eyes should be bright, not sunken. If in doubt, choose frozen fish. This is cleaned and packed almost as soon as it is caught. It is often fresher and contains more nutrients than its fresh counterparts.

1 Preheat the oven to 190°C/375°F/Gas Mark 5. Place the garlic in a small bowl with the lemon rind, juice and olive oil and stir well.

2 Cover and leave to infuse for at least 30 minutes. Stir well before using.

3 Trim the fennel bulb, thinly slice and place in a bowl.

4 Place the cardamom pods in a pestle and mortar and lightly pound to crack the pods.

5 Alternatively, place in a polythene bag and pound gently with a rolling pin. Add the crushed cardamom to the fennel slices.

6 Season the fish with salt and pepper and place on to 4 separate 20.5 x 20.5 cm/8 x 8 inch parchment paper squares.

7 Spoon the fennel mixture over the fish and drizzle with the infused oil.

8 Place the parcels on a baking sheet and bake in the preheated oven for 8–10 minutes or until cooked. Serve immediately in the paper parcels.

1

4

7

Seared Tuna with Pernod & Thyme

INGREDIENTS

Serves 4

4 tuna or swordfish steaks
salt and freshly ground
  black pepper
3 tbsp Pernod
1 tbsp olive oil
zest and juice of 1 lime
2 tsp fresh thyme leaves
4 sun-dried tomatoes

To serve:

freshly cooked mixed rice
tossed green salad

HELPFUL HINT

Tuna is now widely available all year round at fishmongers and in supermarkets. Tuna is an oily fish rich in Omega-3 fatty acids which help in the prevention of heart disease by lowering blood cholesterol levels. Tuna is usually sold in steaks, and the flesh should be dark red in colour.

1. Wipe the fish steaks with a damp cloth or dampened kitchen paper.

2. Season both sides of the fish to taste with salt and pepper, then place in a shallow bowl and reserve.

3. Mix together the Pernod, olive oil, lime zest and juice with the fresh thyme leaves.

4. Finely chop the sun-dried tomatoes and add to the Pernod mixture.

5. Pour the Pernod mixture over the fish and chill in the refrigerator for about 2 hours, spooning the marinade occasionally over the fish.

6. Heat a griddle or heavy-based frying pan. Drain the fish, reserving the marinade. Cook the fish for 3–4 minutes on each side for a steak that is still slightly pink in the middle. Or, if liked, cook the fish for 1–2 minutes longer on each side if you prefer your fish cooked through.

7. Place the remaining marinade in a small saucepan and bring to the boil. Pour the marinade over the fish and serve immediately, with the mixed rice and salad.

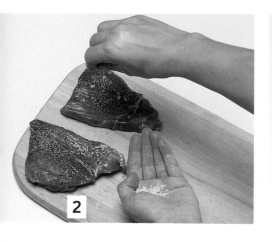

Steamed Monkfish with Chilli & Ginger

INGREDIENTS

Serves 4

700 g/1½ lb skinless monkfish tail
1–2 red chillies
4 cm/1½ inch piece fresh root ginger
1 tsp sesame oil
4 spring onions, trimmed and thinly
   sliced diagonally
2 tbsp soy sauce
2 tbsp Chinese rice wine or dry sherry
freshly steamed rice, to serve

To garnish:
sprigs of fresh coriander
lime wedges

FOOD FACT

Chillies immediately transformed Chinese cooking when they were introduced to China about 100 years ago. They are used extensively in Szechuan and in Hunan.

1 Place the monkfish on a chopping board. Using a sharp knife, cut down each side of the central bone and remove. Cut the fish into 2.5cm/1 inch pieces and reserve.

2 Make a slit down the side of each chilli, remove and discard the seeds and the membrane, then slice thinly. Peel the ginger and either chop finely or grate.

3 Brush a large heatproof plate with the sesame oil and arrange the monkfish pieces in one layer on the plate. Sprinkle over the spring onions and pour over the soy sauce and Chinese rice wine or sherry.

4 Place a wire rack or inverted ramekin in a large wok. Pour in enough water to come about 2.5 cm/1 inch up the side of the wok and bring to the boil over a high heat.

5 Fold a long piece of tinfoil lengthways to about 5–7.5 cm/2–3 inches wide and lay it over the rack or ramekin. It must extend beyond the plate edge when it is placed in the wok.

6 Place the plate with the monkfish on the rack or ramekin and cover tightly. Steam over a medium-low heat for 5 minutes, or until the fish is tender and opaque. Using the tinfoil as a hammock, lift out the plate. Garnish with sprigs of coriander and lime wedges and serve immediately with steamed rice.

2

3

6

Stir–fried Squid with Asparagus

INGREDIENTS

Serves 4

450 g/1 lb squid, cleaned and cut
  into 1 cm/½ inch rings
225 g/8 oz fresh asparagus, sliced
  diagonally into 6.5 cm/
  2½ inch pieces
2 tbsp groundnut oil
2 garlic cloves, peeled and
  thinly sliced
2.5 cm/1 inch piece fresh root ginger,
  peeled and thinly sliced
225 g/8 oz pak choi, trimmed
75 ml/3 fl oz chicken stock
2 tbsp soy sauce
2 tbsp oyster sauce
1 tbsp Chinese rice wine or dry sherry
2 tsp cornflour, blended with
  1 tbsp water
1 tbsp sesame oil
1 tbsp toasted sesame seeds
freshly cooked rice, to serve

TASTY TIP

Pak choi is a member of the
cabbage family. If available, use
baby pak choi for this recipe or
Shanghai pak choi, which is
slightly smaller and more
delicately flavoured.

1 Bring a medium saucepan of water to the boil over a high heat. Add the squid, return to the boil and cook for 30 seconds. Using a wide wok strainer or slotted spoon, transfer to a colander, drain and reserve.

2 Add the asparagus pieces to the boiling water and blanch for 2 minutes. Drain and reserve.

3 Heat a wok or large frying pan, add the groundnut oil and when hot, add the garlic and ginger and stir-fry for 30 seconds. Add the pak choi, stir-fry for 1–2 minutes, then pour in the stock and cook for 1 minute.

4 Blend the soy sauce, oyster sauce and Chinese rice wine or sherry in a bowl or jug, then pour into the wok.

5 Add the reserved squid and asparagus to the wok and stir-fry for 1 minute. Stir the blended cornflour into the wok. Stir-fry for 1 minute, or until the sauce thickens and all the ingredients are well coated.

6 Stir in the sesame oil, give a final stir and turn into a warmed serving dish. Sprinkle with the toasted sesame seeds and serve immediately with freshly cooked rice.

Smoked Haddock Tart

INGREDIENTS

Serves 6

For the shortcrust pastry:

150 g/5 oz plain flour
pinch of salt
25 g/1 oz lard or white vegetable fat,
 cut into small cubes
40 g/1½ oz butter or hard margarine,
 cut into small cubes

For the filling:

225 g/8 oz smoked haddock, skinned
 and cubed
2 large eggs, beaten
300 ml/½ pint double cream
1 tsp Dijon mustard
freshly ground black pepper
125 g/4 oz Gruyère cheese, grated
1 tbsp freshly snipped chives

To serve:

lemon wedges
tomato wedges
fresh green salad leaves

1 Preheat the oven to 190°C/375°F/Gas Mark 5. Sift the flour and salt into a large bowl. Add the fats and mix lightly. Using the fingertips rub into the flour until the mixture resembles breadcrumbs.

2 Sprinkle 1 tablespoon of cold water into the mixture and with a knife, start bringing the dough together. (It may be necessary to use the hands for the final stage.) If the dough does not form a ball instantly, add a little more water.

3 Put the pastry in a polythene bag and chill for at least 30 minutes.

4 On a lightly floured surface, roll out the pastry and use to line a 18 cm/7 inch lightly oiled quiche or flan tin. Prick the base all over with a fork and bake blind in the preheated oven for 15 minutes.

5 Carefully remove the pastry from the oven, brush with a little of the beaten egg.

6 Return to the oven for a further 5 minutes, then place the fish in the pastry case.

7 For the filling, beat together the eggs and cream. Add the mustard, black pepper and cheese and pour over the fish.

8 Sprinkle with the chives and bake for 35–40 minutes or until the filling is golden brown and set in the centre. Serve hot or cold with the lemon and tomato wedges and salad leaves.

2

5

7

Squid & Prawns with Saffron Rice

INGREDIENTS

Serves 4

2 tbsp groundnut oil
1 large onion, peeled and sliced
2 garlic cloves, peeled and chopped
450 g/1 lb tomatoes, skinned,
   deseeded and chopped
225 g/8 oz long-grain rice
¼ tsp saffron strands
600 ml/1 pint fish stock
225 g/8 oz firm fish fillets, such as
   monkfish or cod
225 g/8 oz squid, cleaned
225 g/8 oz mussels with shells
75 g/3 oz frozen or shelled fresh peas
225 g/8 oz peeled prawns, thawed
   if frozen
salt and freshly ground black pepper

To garnish:
8 whole cooked prawns
lemon wedges

1 Heat a large wok, add the oil and when hot, stir-fry the onion and garlic for 3 minutes. Add the tomatoes and continue to stir-fry for 1 minute before adding the rice, saffron and stock. Bring to the boil, reduce the heat, cover and simmer for 10 minutes, stirring occasionally.

2 Meanwhile, remove any skin from the fish fillets, rinse lightly and cut into small cubes. Rinse the squid, pat dry with absorbent kitchen paper, then cut into rings and reserve. Scrub the mussels, discarding any that stay open after being tapped on the work surface. Cover with cold water and reserve until required.

3 Add the peas to the wok together with the fish and return to a gentle simmer. Cover and simmer for 5–10 minutes, or until the rice is tender and most of the liquid has been absorbed.

4 Uncover and stir in the squid, the drained prepared mussels and the peeled prawns. Re-cover and simmer for 5 minutes, or until the mussels have opened. Discard any unopened ones. Season to taste with salt and pepper. Garnish with whole cooked prawns and lemon wedges, then serve immediately.

HELPFUL HINT

Skin tomatoes by making a cross on the top of each one, cover with boiling water, the leave for 2 minutes. Drain and peel.

Prawn Skewers with Tomato Salsa

INGREDIENTS

Serves 4

32 large tiger prawns
olive oil, for brushing
sordalia or aïoli, to serve

For the marinade:

120 ml/4 fl oz extra-virgin olive oil
2 tbsp lemon juice
1 tsp red chilli, finely chopped
1 tsp balsamic vinegar
black pepper

For the tomato salsa:

2 large sun-ripened tomatoes,
    skinned, cored, deseeded
    and chopped
4 spring onions, white parts only,
    very finely chopped
1 red pepper, skinned, deseeded and
    chopped
1 orange or yellow pepper, skinned,
    deseeded and chopped
1 tbsp extra-virgin olive oil
2 tsp balsamic vinegar
4 sprigs fresh basil

1   To make the marinade, place all the ingredients in a non-metallic bowl and whisk together. Set aside.

2   To prepare the prawns, break off the heads. Peel off the shells, leaving the tails intact. Using a small knife, make a slit along the back and remove the thin black vein. Add the prawns to the marinade and stir until well coated. Cover and chill for 15 minutes.

3   Make the salsa. Put all the ingredients, except the basil, in a non-metallic bowl and toss together. Season to taste with salt and pepper.

4   Thread 4 prawns onto a metal skewer, bending each in half. Repeat with 7 more skewers. Brush with marinade.

5   Brush a grill rack with oil. Place the skewers on the rack, then position under a preheated hot grill, about 7.5 cm/3 inches from the heat and cook for 1 minute. Turn the skewers over, brush again and continue to cook for 1–1½ minutes until the prawns turn pink and opaque.

6   Tear the basil leaves and toss with the salsa. Arrange each skewer on a plate with some salsa and garnish with parsley. Serve with skordalia or aïoli dip.

2

3

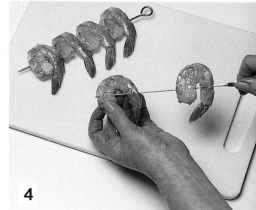

4

Rice with Smoked Salmon & Ginger

INGREDIENTS

Serves 4

225 g/8 oz basmati rice
600 ml/1 pint fish stock
1 bunch spring onions, trimmed
   and diagonally sliced
3 tbsp freshly chopped coriander
1 tsp grated fresh root ginger
200 g/7 oz sliced smoked salmon
2 tbsp soy sauce
1 tsp sesame oil
2 tsp lemon juice
4–6 slices pickled ginger
2 tsp sesame seeds
rocket leaves, to serve

FOOD FACT

Good smoked salmon should look moist and firm and have a peachy pink colour. If you buy it from a delicatessan counter, ask for it to be freshly sliced as any that has already been sliced may be dried out. Vacuum-packed salmon will keep for about 2 weeks in the refrigerator (check the use-by date), but once opened should be used within 3 days.

1 Place the rice in a sieve and rinse under cold water until the water runs clear. Drain, then place in a large saucepan with the stock and bring gently to the boil. Reduce to a simmer and cover with a tight-fitting lid. Cook for 10 minutes, then remove from the heat and leave, covered, for a further 10 minutes.

2 Stir the spring onions, coriander and fresh ginger into the cooked rice and mix well.

3 Spoon the rice into 4 tartlet tins, each measuring 10 cm/4 inches, and press down firmly with the back of a spoon to form cakes. Invert a tin onto an individual serving plate, then tap the base firmly and remove the tin. Repeat with the rest of the filled tins.

4 Top the rice with the salmon, folding if necessary, so the sides of the rice can still be seen in places. Mix together the soy sauce, sesame oil and lemon juice to make a dressing, then drizzle over the salmon. Top with the pickled ginger and a sprinkling of sesame seeds. Scatter the rocket leaves around the edge of the plates and serve immediately.

3

3

4

Salmon & Filo Parcels

INGREDIENTS

Serves 4

1 tbsp sunflower oil

1 bunch of spring onions, trimmed
   and finely chopped

1 tsp paprika

175 g/6 oz long-grain white rice

300 ml/½ pint fish stock

salt and freshly ground black pepper

450 g/1 lb salmon fillet, cubed

1 tbsp freshly chopped parsley

grated rind and juice of 1 lemon

150 g/5 oz rocket

150 g/5 oz spinach

12 sheets filo pastry

50 g/2 oz butter, melted

1. Preheat the oven to 200°C/400°F/Gas Mark 6. Heat the oil in a small frying pan and gently cook the spring onions for 2 minutes. Stir in the paprika and continue to cook for 1 minute, then remove from the heat and reserve.

2. Put the rice in a sieve and rinse under cold running water until the water runs clear; drain. Put the rice and stock in a saucepan, bring to the boil, then cover and simmer for 10 minutes, or until the liquid is absorbed and the rice is tender. Add the spring onion mixture and fork through. Season to taste with salt and pepper, then leave to cool.

3. In a non-metallic bowl, mix together the salmon, parsley, lemon rind and juice and salt and pepper. Reserve.

4. Blanch the rocket and spinach for 30 seconds in a large saucepan of boiling water, or until just wilted. Drain well in a colander and refresh in plenty of cold water, then squeeze out as much moisture as possible.

5. Brush 3 sheets of filo pastry with melted butter and lay them on top of one another. Take a quarter of the rice mixture and arrange it in an oblong in the centre of the pastry. On top of this place a quarter of the salmon followed by a quarter of the rocket and spinach.

6. Draw up the pastry around the filling and twist at the top to create a parcel. Repeat with the remaining pastry and filling until you have 4 parcels. Brush with the remaining butter.

7. Place the parcels on a lightly oiled baking tray and cook in the preheated oven for 20 minutes, or until golden brown and cooked. Serve immediately.

2

1

3

Fish Roulades with Rice & Spinach

INGREDIENTS

Serves 4

4 × 175 g/6 oz lemon sole, skinned
salt and freshly ground black pepper
1 tsp fennel seeds
75 g/3 oz long-grain rice, cooked
150 g/5 oz white crab meat, fresh
  or canned
125 g/4 oz baby spinach, washed
  and trimmed
5 tbsp dry white wine
5 tbsp half-fat crème fraîche
2 tbsp freshly chopped parsley, plus
  extra to garnish
asparagus spears, to serve

1 Wipe each fish fillet with either a clean damp cloth or kitchen paper. Place on a chopping board, skinned side up and season lightly with salt and black pepper.

2 Place the fennel seeds in a pestle and mortar and crush lightly. Transfer to a small bowl and stir in the cooked rice. Drain the crab meat thoroughly. Add to the rice mixture and mix lightly.

3 Lay 2–3 spinach leaves over each fillet and top with a quarter of the crab meat mixture. Roll up and secure with a cocktail stick if necessary. Place into a large pan and pour over the wine. Cover and cook on a medium heat for 5–7 minutes or until cooked.

4 Remove the fish from the cooking liquor, and transfer to a serving plate and keep warm. Stir the crème fraîche into the cooking liquor and season to taste. Heat for 3 minutes, then stir in the chopped parsley.

5 Spoon the sauce on to the base of a plate. Cut each roulade into slices and arrange on top of the sauce. Serve with freshly cooked asparagus spears.

FOOD FACT

Spinach is one of the healthiest, leafy green vegetables to be eaten. It also acts as an antioxidant and it is suggested that it can reduce risks of certain cancers. Why not use whole-grain rice to add nutritional value and to give the dish a nuttier taste?

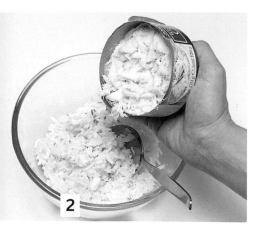

2

3

4

Orange Roasted Whole Chicken

INGREDIENTS

Serves 6

1 small orange, thinly sliced
50 g/2 oz sugar
1.4 kg/3 lb oven-ready chicken
1 small bunch fresh coriander
1 small bunch fresh mint
2 tbsp olive oil
1 tsp Chinese five spice powder
½ tsp paprika
1 tsp fennel seeds, crushed
salt and freshly ground black pepper
sprigs of fresh coriander, to garnish
freshly cooked vegetables, to serve

TASTY TIP

To make oven-baked rice, soften a chopped onion in 1 tablespoon sunflower oil in an ovenproof casserole. Stir in 250 g/9 oz long-grain rice, then remove from the heat. Pour in 750 ml/1¼ pints chicken or vegetable stock, 1 star anise, ½ cinnamon stick, 1 bay leaf, salt and pepper. Cover and cook for 45 minutes or until tender. Fluff up with a fork and remove the spices.

1 Preheat the oven to 190°C/375°F/Gas Mark 5, 10 minutes before cooking. Place the orange slices in a small saucepan, cover with water, bring to the boil, then simmer for 2 minutes and drain. Place the sugar in a clean saucepan with 150 ml/¼ pint fresh water. Stir over a low heat until the sugar dissolves, then bring to the boil, add the drained orange slices and simmer for 10 minutes. Remove from the heat and leave in the syrup until cold.

2 Remove any excess fat from inside the chicken. Starting at the neck end, carefully loosen the skin of the chicken over the breast and legs without tearing. Push the orange slices under the loosened skin with the coriander and mint.

3 Mix together the olive oil, Chinese five spice powder, paprika and crushed fennel seeds and season to taste with salt and pepper. Brush the chicken skin generously with this mixture. Transfer to a wire rack set over a roasting tin and roast in the preheated oven for 1½ hours, or until the juices run clear when a skewer is inserted into the thickest part of the thigh. Remove from the oven and leave to rest for 10 minutes. Garnish with sprigs of fresh coriander and serve with freshly cooked vegetables.

1

2

3

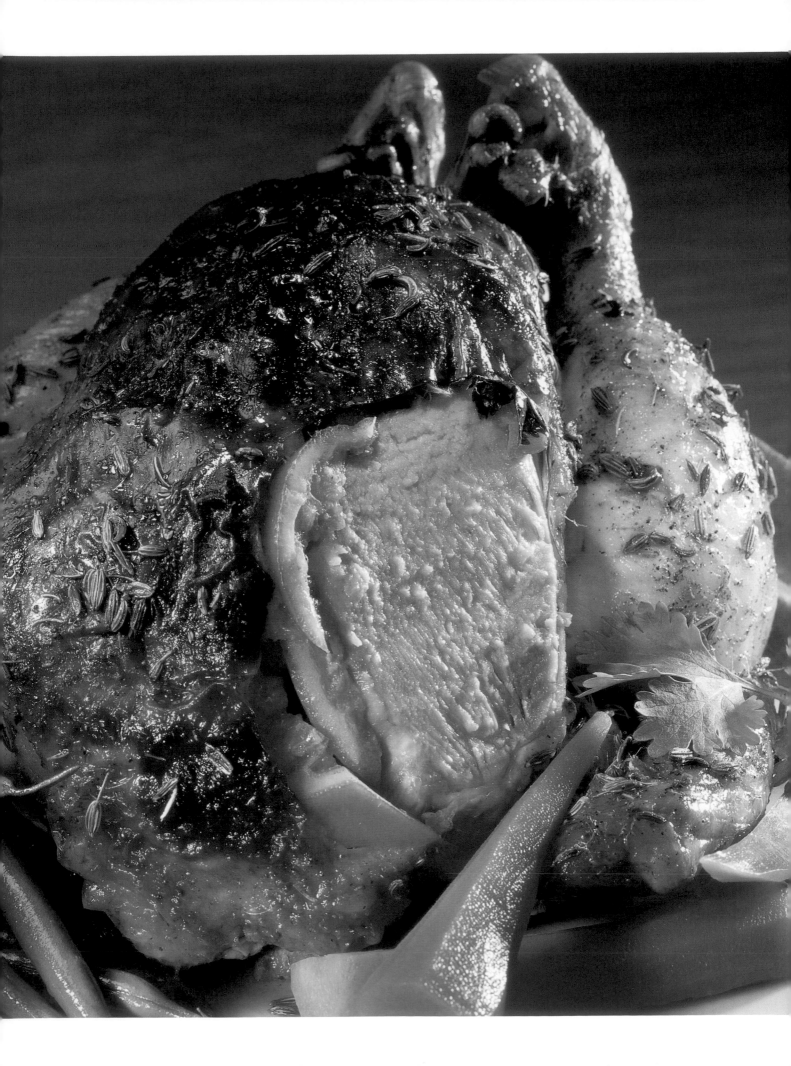

Roast Chicken with Ginger & Lime

INGREDIENTS

Serves 4

3 cm/1 inch piece fresh ginger root,
    finely chopped
2 garlic cloves, finely chopped
1 small onion, finely chopped
1 lemon grass stalk, finely chopped
½ tsp salt
1 tsp black peppercorns
1.5 kg/3 lb 5 oz roasting chicken
1 tbsp coconut cream
2 tbsp lime juice
2 tbsp clear honey
1 tsp cornflour
2 tsp water
stir-fried vegetables, to serve

1 Put the ginger, garlic, onion, lemon grass, salt and peppercorns in a pestle and mortar and crush to form a smooth paste.

2 Cut the chicken in half lengthways, using poultry shears or strong kitchen scissors. Spread the paste all over the chicken, both inside and out, and spread it on to the flesh under the breast skin. Cover and chill overnight, or at least several hours.

3 In a small pan, heat the coconut cream, lime juice and honey together, stirring until smooth. Brush a little of the mixture evenly over the chicken.

4 Place the chicken halves on a tray over a roasting tin half-filled with boiling water. Roast in an oven preheated to 180°C/ 350°F/Gas Mark 4 for about 1 hour, or until the chicken is a rich golden brown, basting occasionally with the reserved lime and honey mixture.

5 When the chicken is cooked, boil the water from the roasting tin to reduce it to about 100 ml/3½ fl oz. Blend the cornflour and water and stir into the reduced liquid. Heat gently to the boil, then stir until slightly thickened and clear. Serve the chicken with the sauce and stir-fried vegetables.

1

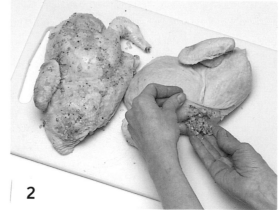

2

5

Sauvignon Chicken & Mushroom Filo Pie

INGREDIENTS

Serves 4

1 onion, peeled and chopped
1 leek, trimmed and chopped
225 ml/8 fl oz chicken stock
3 x 175 g/6 oz chicken breasts
150 ml/¼ pint dry white wine
1 bay leaf
175 g/6 oz baby
  button mushrooms
2 tbsp plain flour
1 tbsp freshly chopped tarragon
salt and freshly ground black pepper
sprig of fresh parsley, to garnish
seasonal vegetables, to serve

For the topping:

75 g/3 oz (about 5 sheets)
  filo pastry
1 tbsp sunflower oil
1 tsp sesame seeds

1 Preheat the oven to 190°C/375°F/Gas Mark 5. Put the onion and leek in a heavy-based saucepan with 125 ml/4 fl oz of the stock.

2 Bring to the boil, cover and simmer for 5 minutes, then uncover and cook until all the stock has evaporated and the vegetables are tender.

3 Cut the chicken into bite-sized cubes. Add to the pan with the remaining stock, wine and bay leaf. Cover and gently simmer for 5 minutes. Add the mushrooms and simmer for a further 5 minutes.

4 Blend the flour with 3 tablespoons of cold water. Stir into the pan and cook, stirring all the time until the sauce has thickened.

5 Stir the tarragon into the sauce and season with salt and pepper.

6 Spoon the mixture into a 1.2 litre/2 pint pie dish, discarding the bay leaf.

7 Lightly brush a sheet of filo pastry with a little of the oil.

8 Crumple the pastry slightly. Arrange on top of the filling. Repeat with the remaining filo sheets and oil, then sprinkle the top of the pie with the sesame seeds.

9 Bake the pie on the middle shelf of the preheated oven for 20 minutes until the filo pastry topping is golden and crisp. Garnish with a sprig of parsley. Serve the pie immediately with the seasonal vegetables.

3

6

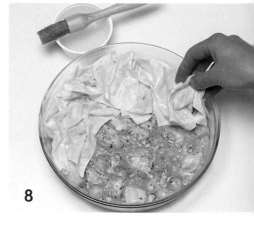

8

Guinea Fowl with Calvados & Apples

INGREDIENTS

Serves 4

4 guinea fowl supremes, each
  about 150 g/5 oz, skinned
1 tbsp plain flour
1 tbsp sunflower oil
1 onion, peeled and finely sliced
1 garlic clove, peeled and crushed
1 tsp freshly chopped thyme
150 ml/¼ pint dry cider

salt and freshly ground
  black pepper
3 tbsp Calvados brandy
sprigs of fresh thyme, to garnish

For the caramalised apples:

15 g/½ oz unsalted butter
2 red-skinned eating apples,
  quartered, cored and sliced
1 tsp caster sugar

1 Lightly dust the guinea fowl supremes with the flour.

2 Heat 2 teaspoons of the oil in a large non-stick frying pan and cook the supremes for 2–3 minutes on each side until browned. Remove from the pan and reserve.

3 Heat the remaining teaspoon of oil in the pan and add the onion and garlic. Cook over a medium heat for 10 minutes, stirring occasionally until soft and just beginning to colour.

4 Stir in the chopped thyme and cider. Return the guinea fowl to the pan, season with salt and pepper and bring to a very gentle simmer. Cover and cook over a low heat for 15–20 minutes or until the guinea fowl is tender.

5 Remove the guinea fowl and keep warm. Turn up the heat and boil the sauce until thickened and reduced by half.

6 Meanwhile, prepare the caramelised apples. Melt the butter in a small non-stick pan, add the apple slices in a single layer and sprinkle with the sugar. Cook until the apples are tender and beginning to caramelise, turning once.

7 Put the Calvados in a metal ladle or small saucepan and gently heat until warm. Carefully set alight with a match, let the flames die down, then stir into the sauce.

8 Serve the guinea fowl with the sauce spooned over and garnished with the caramelised apples and sprigs of fresh thyme.

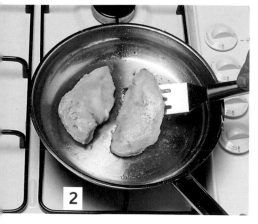

2

4

7

Chicken with Roasted Fennel & Citrus Rice

INGREDIENTS

Serves 4

2 tsp fennel seeds
1 tbsp freshly chopped oregano
1 garlic clove, peeled and crushed
salt and freshly ground black pepper
4 chicken quarters,
   about 175 g/6 oz each
½ lemon, finely sliced
1 fennel bulb, trimmed
2 tsp olive oil
4 plum tomatoes
25 g/1 oz stoned green olives

To garnish:
fennel fronds,
orange slices

For the citrus rice:
225 g/8 oz long-grain rice
finely grated rind and juice
   of ½ lemon
150 ml/¼ pint orange juice
450 ml/¾ pint boiling chicken
   or vegetable stock

1 Preheat the oven to 200°C/400°F/Gas Mark 6. Lightly crush the fennel seeds and mix with oregano, garlic, salt and pepper. Place between the skin and flesh of the chicken breasts, careful not to tear the skin. Arrange the lemon slices on top of the chicken.

2 Cut the fennel into 8 wedges. Place on baking tray with the chicken. Lightly brush the fennel with the oil. Cook the chicken and fennel on the top shelf of the preheated oven for 10 minutes.

3 Meanwhile, put the rice in a 2.3 litre/4 pint ovenproof dish. Stir in the lemon rind and juice, orange juice and stock. Cover with a lid and put on the middle shelf of the oven.

4 Reduce the oven temperature to 180°C/350°F/Gas Mark 4. Cook the chicken for a further 40 minutes, turning the fennel wedges and lemon slices once. Deseed and chop the tomatoes. Add to the tray and cook for 5–10 minutes. Remove from the oven.

5 When cooled slightly, remove the chicken skin and discard. Fluff the rice, scatter olives over the dish. Garnish with fennel fronds, orange slices and serve.

1

3

4

Turkey Escalopes with Apricot Chutney

INGREDIENTS

Serves 4

4 x 175–225 g/6–8 oz turkey steaks
1 tbsp plain flour
salt and freshly ground black pepper
1 tbsp olive oil
flat-leaf parsley sprigs, to garnish
orange wedges, to serve

For the apricot chutney:

125 g/4 oz no-need-to-soak dried
   apricots, chopped
1 red onion, peeled and
   finely chopped
1 tsp grated fresh root ginger
2 tbsp caster sugar
finely grated rind of ½ orange
125 ml/4 fl oz fresh orange juice
125 ml/4 fl oz ruby port
1 whole clove

1   Put a turkey steak onto a sheet of non-pvc clingfilm or non-stick baking parchment. Cover with a second sheet.

2   Using a rolling pin, gently pound the turkey until the meat is flattened to about 5 mm/¼ inch thick. Repeat to make 4 escalopes.

3   Mix the flour with the salt and pepper and use to lightly dust the turkey escalopes.

4   Put the turkey escalopes on a board or baking tray and cover with a piece of non-pvc clingfilm or non-stick baking parchment. Chill in the refrigerator until ready to cook.

5   For the apricot chutney, put the apricots, onion, ginger, sugar, orange rind, orange juice, port and clove into a saucepan.

6   Slowly bring to the boil and simmer, uncovered for 10 minutes, stirring occasionally, until thick and syrupy.

7   Remove the clove and stir in the chopped coriander.

8   Heat the oil in a pan and chargriddle the turkey escalopes, in two batches if necessary, for 3–4 minutes on each side until golden brown and tender.

9   Spoon the chutney onto four individual serving plates. Place a turkey escalope on top of each spoonful of chutney. Garnish with sprigs of parsley and serve immediately with orange wedges.

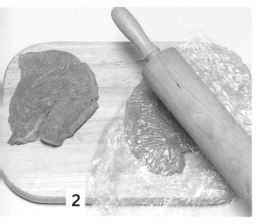
2

5

8

Duck with Berry Sauce

INGREDIENTS

Serves 4

4 x 175 g/6 oz boneless
   duck breasts
salt and freshly ground
   black pepper
1 tsp sunflower oil

For the sauce:

juice of 1 orange
1 bay leaf
3 tbsp redcurrant jelly
150 g/5 oz fresh or frozen
   mixed berries
2 tbsp dried cranberries or cherries
½ tsp soft light brown sugar
1 tbsp balsamic vinegar
1 tsp freshly chopped mint
sprigs of fresh mint, to garnish

To serve:

freshly cooked potatoes
freshly cooked green beans

HELPFUL HINT

Duck breasts are best served slightly pink in the middle. Whole ducks, however, should be thoroughly cooked.

1 Remove the skins from the duck breasts and season with a little salt and pepper. Brush a griddle pan with the oil, then heat on the stove until smoking hot.

2 Place the duck, skinned-side down in the pan. Cook over a medium-high heat for 5 minutes, or until well browned. Turn the duck and cook for 2 minutes. Lower the heat and cook for a further 5–8 minutes, or until cooked, but still slightly pink in the centre. Remove from the pan and keep warm.

3 While the duck is cooking, make the sauce. Put the orange juice, bay leaf, redcurrant jelly, fresh or frozen and dried berries and sugar in a small griddle pan. Add any juices left in the griddle pan to the small pan. Slowly bring to the boil, lower the heat and simmer uncovered for 4–5 minutes, until the fruit is soft.

4 Remove the bay leaf. Stir in the vinegar and chopped mint and season to taste with salt and pepper.

5 Slice the duck breasts on the diagonal and arrange on serving plates. Spoon over the berry sauce and garnish with sprigs of fresh mint. Serve immediately with the potatoes and green beans.

Sticky–glazed Spatchcocked Poussins

INGREDIENTS

Serves 4

2 poussins, each about 700 g/1½ lb
salt and freshly ground black pepper
4 kumquats, thinly sliced
assorted salad leaves, crusty bread
  or new potatoes, to serve

For the glaze:

zest of 1 small lemon, finely grated
1 tbsp lemon juice
1 tbsp dry sherry
2 tbsp clear honey
2 tbsp dark soy sauce
2 tbsp whole-grain mustard
1 tsp tomato purée
½ tsp Chinese five spice powder

1 Preheat the grill just before cooking. Place one of the poussins breast-side down on a board. Using poultry shears, cut down one side of the backbone. Cut down the other side of the backbone. Remove the bone.

2 Open out the poussin and press down hard on the breast bone with the heel of your hand to break it and to flatten the poussin.

3 Thread two skewers crosswise through the bird to keep it flat, ensuring that each skewer goes through a wing and out through the leg on the opposite side. Repeat with the other bird. Season both sides of the bird with salt and pepper.

4 To make the glaze, mix together the lemon zest and juice, sherry, honey, soy sauce, mustard, tomato purée and Chinese five spice powder and use to brush all over the poussins.

5 Place the poussins skin-side down on a grill rack and grill under a medium heat for 15 minutes, brushing halfway through with more glaze.

6 Turn the poussins over and grill for 10 minutes. Brush again with glaze and arrange the kumquat slices on top. Grill for a further 15 minutes until well-browned and cooked through. If they start to brown too quickly, turn down the grill a little.

7 Remove the skewers and cut each poussin in half along the breastbone. Serve immediately with the salad, crusty bread or new potatoes.

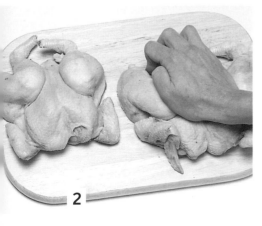

2

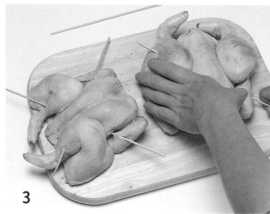

3

6

Chicken & White Wine Risotto

INGREDIENTS

Serves 4–6

2 tbsp oil

125 g/4 oz unsalted butter

2 shallots, peeled and finely chopped

300 g/11 oz Arborio rice

600 ml/1 pint dry white wine

750 ml/1¼ pints chicken
  stock, heated

350 g/12 oz skinless chicken breast
  fillets, thinly sliced

50 g/2 oz Parmesan cheese, grated

2 tbsp freshly chopped dill or parsley

salt and freshly ground black pepper

1 Heat the oil and half the butter in a large heavy-based saucepan over a medium-high heat. Add the shallots and cook for 2 minutes, or until softened, stirring frequently. Add the rice and cook for 2–3 minutes, stirring frequently, until the rice is translucent and well coated.

2 Pour in half the wine; it will bubble and steam rapidly. Cook, stirring constantly, until the liquid is absorbed. Add a ladleful of the hot stock and cook until the liquid is absorbed. Carefully stir in the chicken.

3 Continue adding the stock, about half a ladleful at a time, allowing each addition to be absorbed before adding the next; never allow the rice to cook dry. This process should take about 20 minutes. The risotto should have a creamy consistency and the rice should be tender, but firm to the bite.

4 Stir in the remaining wine and cook for 2–3 minutes. Remove from the heat and stir in the remaining butter with the Parmesan cheese and half the chopped herbs. Season to taste with salt and pepper. Spoon into warmed shallow bowls and sprinkle each with the remaining chopped herbs. Serve immediately.

HELPFUL HINT

Keep the stock to be added to the risotto at a low simmer in a separate saucepan, so that it is piping hot when added to the rice. This will ensure that the dish is kept at a constant heat during cooking, which is important to achieve a perfect creamy texture.

Potato-stuffed Roast Poussin

INGREDIENTS

Serves 4

4 oven-ready poussins

salt and freshly ground black pepper

1 lemon, cut into quarters

450 g/1 lb floury potatoes, peeled and
  cut into 4 cm/1½ inch pieces

1 tbsp freshly chopped thyme
  or rosemary

3–4 tbsp olive oil

4 garlic cloves, unpeeled and
  lightly smashed

8 slices streaky bacon or Parma ham

125 ml/4 fl oz white wine

2 spring onions, trimmed and
  thinly sliced

2 tbsp double cream or crème fraîche

lemon wedges, to garnish

1 Preheat the oven to 220°C/425°F/Gas Mark 7. Place a roasting tin in the oven to heat. Rinse the poussin cavities and pat dry with absorbent kitchen paper. Season the cavities with salt and pepper and a squeeze of lemon. Push a lemon quarter into each cavity.

2 Put the potatoes in a saucepan of lightly salted water and bring to the boil. Reduce the heat to low and simmer until just tender; do not overcook. Drain and cool slightly. Sprinkle the chopped herbs over the potatoes and drizzle with 2–3 tablespoons of the oil.

3 Spoon half the seasoned potatoes into the poussin cavities; do not pack too tightly. Rub each poussin with a little more oil and season with pepper. Carefully spoon 1 tablespoon of oil into the hot roasting tin and arrange the poussins in the tin. Spoon the remaining potatoes around the edge. Sprinkle over the garlic.

4 Roast the poussins in the preheated oven for 30 minutes, or until the skin is golden and beginning to crisp. Carefully lay the bacon slices over the breast of each poussin and continue to roast for 15–20 minutes until crisp and the poussins are cooked through.

5 Transfer the poussins and potatoes to a serving platter and cover loosely with tinfoil. Skim off the fat from the juices. Place the tin over a medium heat, add the wine and spring onions. Cook briefly, scraping the bits from the bottom of the tin. Whisk in the cream or crème fraîche and bubble for 1 minute, or until thickened. Garnish the poussins with lemon wedges, and serve with the creamy gravy.

2

3

4

Spicy Chicken with Open Ravioli & Tomato Sauce

INGREDIENTS

Serves 2–3

2 tbsp olive oil
1 onion, peeled and finely chopped
1 tsp ground cumin
1 tsp hot paprika pepper
1 tsp ground cinnamon
175 g/6 oz boneless and skinless
  chicken breasts, chopped
salt and freshly ground black pepper
1 tbsp smooth peanut butter
50 g/2 oz butter
1 shallot, peeled and finely chopped
2 garlic cloves, peeled and crushed
400 g can chopped tomatoes
125 g/4 oz fresh egg lasagne
2 tbsp freshly chopped coriander

1 Heat the olive oil in a frying pan, add the onion and cook gently for 2–3 minutes then add the cumin, paprika pepper and cinnamon and cook for a further 1 minute. Add the chicken, season to taste with salt and pepper and cook for 3–4 minutes, or until tender. Add the peanut butter and stir until well mixed and reserve.

2 Melt the butter in the frying pan, add the shallot and cook for 2 minutes. Add the tomatoes and garlic and season to taste. Simmer gently for 20 minutes, or until thickened, then keep the sauce warm.

3 Cut each sheet of lasagne into 6 squares. Bring a large pan of lightly salted water to a rolling boil. Add the lasagne squares and cook according to the packet instructions, about 3–4 minutes, or until 'al dente'. Drain the lasagne pieces thoroughly, reserve and keep warm.

4 Layer the pasta squares with the spicy filling on individual warmed plates. Pour over a little of the hot tomato sauce and sprinkle with chopped coriander. Serve immediately.

HELPFUL HINT

Because fresh pasta contains fresh eggs it should always be stored in the refrigerator, kept in its packet or wrapped in non-stick baking parchment, then in clingfilm.

1

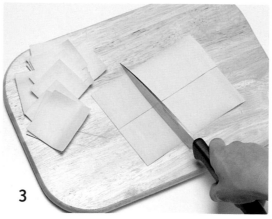
3

4

Garlic Mushrooms with Crispy Bacon & Chicken Liver Sauté

INGREDIENTS

Serves 4

4 large field mushrooms

40 g/1½ oz butter, melted and cooled

2 garlic cloves, peeled and crushed

1 tbsp sunflower oil

3 rashers smoked streaky bacon,
  derinded and chopped

4 shallots, peeled and thinly sliced

450 g/1 lb chicken livers, halved

2 tbsp marsala or sweet sherry

4 tbsp chicken or vegetable stock

6 tbsp double cream

2 tsp freshly chopped thyme

salt and freshly ground black pepper

FOOD FACT

Mushrooms are an extremely nutritious food, rich in vitamins and minerals, which help to boost our immune system. This recipe could be adapted to include shitake mushrooms which can significantly boost and protect the body's immune system and can go some way to boost the body's protection against cancer.

1 Remove the stalks from the mushrooms and roughly chop. Mix together 25 g/1 oz of the butter and garlic and brush over both sides of the mushroom caps. Place on the rack of a grill pan.

2 Heat a wok, add the oil and when hot, add the bacon and stir-fry for 2–3 minutes, or until crispy. Remove and reserve. Add the remaining butter to the wok and stir-fry the shallots and chopped mushroom stalks for 4–5 minutes until they are softened.

3 Add the chicken livers and cook for 3–4 minutes, or until well browned on the outside, but still pink and tender inside. Pour in the marsala or sherry and the stock. Simmer for 1 minute, then stir in the cream, thyme, salt and pepper and half the bacon. Cook for about 30 seconds to heat through.

4 While the livers are frying, cook the mushroom caps under a hot grill for 3–4 minutes each side, until tender.

5 Place the mushrooms on warmed serving plates, allowing 1 per person. Spoon the chicken livers over and around the mushrooms. Scatter with the remaining bacon and serve immediately.

1

2

3

Pork Loin Stuffed with Orange & Hazelnut Rice

INGREDIENTS

Serves 4

15 g/½ oz butter
1 shallot, peeled and finely chopped
50 g/2 oz long-grain brown rice
175 ml/6 fl oz vegetable stock
½ orange
25 g/1 oz ready-to-eat dried prunes,
   stoned and chopped
25 g/1 oz hazelnuts, roasted and
   roughly chopped
1 small egg, beaten
1 tbsp freshly chopped parsley
salt and freshly ground pepper
450 g/1 lb boneless pork tenderloin or
   fillet, trimmed

To serve:
steamed courgettes
carrots

1 Preheat the oven to 190°C/375°F/Gas Mark 5, 10 minutes before required. Heat the butter in a small saucepan, add the shallot and cook gently for 2–3 minutes until softened. Add the rice and stir well for 1 minute. Add the stock, stir well and bring to the boil. Cover tightly and simmer gently for 30 minutes until the rice is tender and all the liquid is absorbed. Leave to cool.

2 Grate the orange rind and reserve. Remove the white pith and chop the orange flesh finely. Mix together the orange rind and flesh, prunes, hazelnuts, cooled rice, egg and parsley. Season to taste with salt and pepper.

3 Cut the fillet in half, then using a sharp knife, split the pork fillet lengthways almost in two, forming a pocket, leaving it just attached. Open out the pork and put between 2 pieces of clingfilm. Flatten using a meat mallet until about half its original thickness. Spoon the filling into the pocket and close the fillet over. Tie along the length with kitchen string at regular intervals.

4 Put the pork fillet in a small roasting tray and cook in the top of the preheated oven for 25–30 minutes, or until the meat is just tender. Remove from the oven and allow to rest for 5 minutes. Slice into rounds and serve with steamed courgettes and carrots.

TASTY TIP
For an alternative stuffing try adding pine nuts and thyme.

2

3

3

Seared Calves' Liver with Onions & Mustard Mash

INGREDIENTS

Serves 2

2 tbsp olive oil

100 g/3½ oz butter

3 large onions, peeled and
  finely sliced

pinch of sugar

salt and freshly ground black pepper

1 tbsp sprigs of fresh thyme

1 tbsp balsamic vinegar

700 g/1½ lb potatoes, peeled and cut
  into chunks

6–8 tbsp milk

1 tbsp wholegrain mustard

3–4 fresh sage leaves

550 g/1¼ lb thinly sliced calves' liver

1 tsp lemon juice

HELPFUL HINT

Lambs' liver may be used for this recipe instead, but tone down the slightly stronger flavour by soaking in milk for up to 1 hour before cooking.

1 Preheat the oven to 150°C/300°F/Gas Mark 2. Heat half the oil and 25 g/1 oz of the butter in a flameproof casserole. When foaming, add the onions. Cover and cook over a low heat for 20 minutes until softened and beginning to collapse. Add the sugar and season with salt and pepper. Stir in the thyme. Cover the casserole and transfer to the preheated oven. Cook for a further 30–45 minutes until softened completely, but not browned. Remove from the oven and stir in the balsamic vinegar.

2 Meanwhile, boil the potatoes in boiling salted water for 15–18 minutes until tender. Drain well, then return to the pan. Place over a low heat to dry completely, remove from the heat and stir in 50 g/ 2 oz of the butter, the milk, mustard and salt and pepper to taste. Mash thoroughly until creamy and keep warm.

3 Heat a large frying pan and add the remaining butter and oil. When it is foaming, add the mustard and sage leaves and stir for a few seconds, then add the liver. Cook over a high heat for 1–2 minutes on each side. It should remain slightly pink: do not overcook. Remove the liver from the pan. Add the lemon juice to the pan and swirl around to deglaze.

4 To serve, place a large spoonful of the mashed potato on each plate. Top with some of the melting onions, the liver and finally the pan juices.

Fettuccine with Calves' Liver & Calvados

INGREDIENTS

Serves 4

450 g/1 lb calves' liver, trimmed and
　thinly sliced
50 g/2 oz plain flour
salt and freshly ground black pepper
1 tsp paprika
50 g/2 oz butter
11½ tbsp olive oil
2 tbsp Calvados
150 ml/¼ pint cider
150 ml/¼ pint whipping cream
350 g/12 oz fresh fettuccine
fresh thyme sprigs, to garnish

HELPFUL HINT

Calvados is made from apples and adds a fruity taste to this dish, although you can, of course, use ordinary brandy instead. Calves' liver is very tender, with a delicate flavour. It should be cooked over a high heat until the outside is brown and crusty and the centre still slightly pink.

1 Season the flour with the salt, black pepper and paprika, then toss the liver in the flour until well coated.

2 Melt half the butter and 1 tablespoon of the olive oil in a large frying pan and fry the liver in batches for 1 minute, or until just browned but still slightly pink inside. Remove using a slotted spoon and place in a warmed dish.

3 Add the remaining butter to the pan, stir in 1 tablespoon of the seasoned flour and cook for 1 minute. Pour in the Calvados and cider and cook over a high heat for 30 seconds. Stir the cream into the sauce and simmer for 1 minute to thicken slightly, then season to taste. Return the liver to the pan and heat through.

4 Bring a large pan of lightly salted water to a rolling boil. Add the fettuccine and cook according to the packet instructions, about 3–4 minutes, or until 'al dente'.

5 Drain the fettuccine thoroughly, return to the pan and toss in the remaining olive oil. Divide among 4 warmed plates and spoon the liver and sauce over the pasta. Garnish with thyme sprigs and serve immediately.

1

3

3

Red Wine Risotto with Lambs' Kidneys & Caramelised Shallots

INGREDIENTS

Serves 4

8 lambs' kidneys, halved and
  cores removed
150 ml/¼ pint milk
2 tbsp olive oil
50 g/2 oz butter
275 g/10 oz shallots, peeled and
  halved if large
1 onion, peeled and finely chopped
2 garlic cloves, peeled and
  finely chopped
350 g/12 oz Arborio rice
225 ml/8 fl oz red wine
1 litre/13¾ pints chicken or vegetable
  stock, heated
1 tbsp sprigs of fresh thyme
50 g/2 oz Parmesan cheese, grated
salt and freshly ground black pepper
fresh herbs, to garnish

1 Place the lambs' kidneys in a bowl and pour the milk over. Leave to soak for 15–20 minutes, then drain and pat dry on absorbent kitchen paper. Discard the milk.

2 Heat 1 tablespoon of the oil with 25 g/1 oz of the butter in a medium saucepan. Add the shallots, cover and cook for 10 minutes over a gentle heat. Remove the lid and cook for a further 10 minutes, or until tender and golden.

3 Meanwhile, heat the remaining oil with the remaining butter in a deep-sided frying pan. Add the onion and cook over a medium heat for 5–7 minutes until starting to brown. Add the garlic and cook briefly.

4 Stir in the rice and cook for a further minute until glossy and well coated in oil and butter. Add half the red wine and stir until absorbed. Add a ladleful or two of the stock and stir well until the stock is absorbed. Continue adding the stock, a ladleful at a time, and stirring well between additions, until all of the stock is added and the rice is just tender, but still firm. Remove from the heat.

5 Meanwhile, when the rice is nearly cooked, increase the heat under the shallots, add the thyme and kidneys. Cook for 3–4 minutes, then add the wine.

6 Bring to the boil, then simmer rapidly until the red wine is reduced and syrupy. Stir the cheese into the rice with the caramelised shallots and kidneys. Season to taste, garnish and serve.

1

4

5

Brandied Lamb Chops

INGREDIENTS

Serves 4

8 lamb loin chops
3 tbsp groundnut oil
5 cm/2 inch piece fresh root ginger,
   peeled and cut into matchsticks
2 garlic cloves, peeled and chopped
225 g/8 oz button mushrooms, wiped
   and halved if large
2 tbsp light soy sauce
2 tbsp dry sherry
1 tbsp brandy
1 tsp Chinese five spice powder
1 tsp soft brown sugar
200 ml/7 fl oz lamb or chicken stock
1 tsp sesame oil

To serve:
freshly cooked rice
freshly stir-fried vegetables

1   Using a sharp knife, trim the lamb chops, discarding any sinew or fat. Heat a wok or large frying pan, add the oil and when hot, add the lamb chops and cook for 3 minutes on each side or until browned. Using a fish slice, transfer the lamb chops to a plate and keep warm.

2   Add the ginger, garlic and button mushrooms to the wok and stir-fry for 3 minutes or until the mushrooms have browned.

3   Return the lamb chops to the wok together with the soy sauce, sherry, brandy, five spice powder and sugar. Pour in the stock, bring to the boil, then reduce the heat slightly and simmer for 4–5 minutes, or until the lamb is tender, ensuring that the liquid does not evaporate completely. Add the sesame oil and heat for a further 30 seconds. Turn into a warmed serving dish and serve immediately with freshly cooked rice and stir-fried vegetables.

FOOD FACT
Lamb is not widely eaten in China, but Chinese Muslims (who are forbidden to eat pork) often cook it as do Mongols and people from Sinkiang.

Beef & Red Wine Pie

INGREDIENTS

Serves 4

1 quantity quick flaky pastry
  (see page 66), chilled
700 g/1½ lb stewing
  beef, cubed
4 tbsp seasoned plain flour
2 tbsp sunflower oil
2 onions, peeled and chopped
2 garlic cloves, peeled and crushed
1 tbsp freshly chopped thyme
300 ml/½ pint red wine
150 ml/¼ pint beef stock
1–2 tsp Worcestershire sauce
2 tbsp tomato ketchup
2 bay leaves
a knob of butter
225 g/8 oz button mushrooms
beaten egg or milk, to glaze
sprig of parsley, to garnish

HELPFUL HINT

Shortcrust or puff pastry could also be used to top the pie in this recipe. It is important though, whichever pastry is used, to brush the pie with beaten egg or milk before baking, as this will result in an appetising golden crust.

1 Preheat the oven to 200°C/400°F/Gas Mark 6. Toss the beef cubes in the seasoned flour.

2 Heat the oil in a large heavy-based frying pan. Fry the beef in batches for about 5 minutes until golden brown.

3 Return all of the beef to the pan and add the onions, garlic and thyme. Fry for about 10 minutes, stirring occasionally. If the beef begins to stick, add a little water.

4 Add the red wine and stock and bring to the boil. Stir in the Worcestershire sauce, tomato ketchup and bay leaves.

5 Cover and simmer on a very low heat for about 1 hour or until the beef is tender.

6 Heat the butter and gently sauté the mushrooms until golden brown. Add to the stew. Simmer uncovered for a further 15 minutes. Remove the bay leaves. Spoon the beef into a 1.1 litre/2 pint pie dish and reserve.

7 Roll out the pastry on a lightly floured surface. Cut out the lid to 5 mm/¼ inch wider than the dish. Brush the rim with the beaten egg and lay the pastry lid on top. Press to seal, then knock the edges with the back of the knife.

8 Cut a slit in the lid and brush with the beaten egg or milk to glaze. Bake in the preheated oven for 30 minutes, or until golden brown. Garnish with the sprig of parsley and serve immediately.

2

4

8

Lamb Skewers on Rosemary

INGREDIENTS

Serves 4

500 g/1 lb 2 oz boneless leg of lamb
4 long, thick branches fresh rosemary
1 or 2 red peppers, depending
  on the size
12 large garlic cloves, peeled
olive oil
Spiced Pilau with Saffron, to serve

For the marinade:

2 tbsp olive oil
2 tbsp dry white wine
$1/2$ tsp ground cumin
1 sprig fresh oregano, chopped

1   At least 4 hours before cooking, cut the lamb into 5 cm/2 inch cubes. Mix all the marinade ingredients together in a bowl. Add the lamb cubes, stir well to coat and leave to marinate for at least 4 hours, or up to 12.

2   An hour before cooking, put the rosemary in a bowl of cold water and leave to soak.

3   Slice the tops off the peppers, cut them in half, quarter and remove the cores and seeds. Cut the halves into 5 cm/2 inch pieces.

4   Bring a small saucepan of water to the boil, blanch the pepper pieces and garlic cloves for 1 minute. Drain and refresh under cold water. Pat dry and set aside.

5   Remove the rosemary from the water and pat dry. To make the skewers, remove the rosemary needles from about the first 4 cm/ $1^3/_4$ inches of the branches so you have a 'handle' to turn them over with while grilling.

6   Thread alternate pieces of lamb, garlic and red pepper pieces on to the 4 rosemary skewers: the meat should be tender enough to push the sprig through it, but, if not, use a metal skewer to poke a hole in the centre of each cube.

7   Lightly oil the grill rack. Place the skewers on the rack about 12.5 cm/5 inches under a preheated hot grill and grill for 10–12 minutes, brushing with any leftover marinade or olive oil and turning, until the meat is cooked. Serve with the pilau.

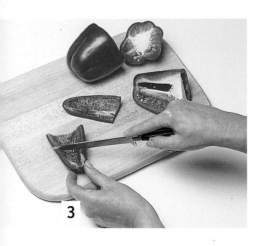

3

5

6

Leg of Lamb with Minted Rice

INGREDIENTS

Serves 4

1 tbsp olive oil
1 medium onion, peeled and
   finely chopped
1 garlic clove, peeled and crushed
1 celery stalk, trimmed and chopped
1 large mild red chilli, deseeded
   and chopped
75 g/3 oz long-grain rice
150 ml/¼ pint lamb or chicken stock
2 tbsp freshly chopped mint
salt and freshly ground black pepper
1.4 kg/3 lb boned leg of lamb
freshly cooked vegetables, to serve

HELPFUL HINT

Use a meat thermometer to check whether the joint is cooked, or push a fine skewer into the thickest part: for rare meat the juices will be slightly red, for medium they will be pink and when well-done, the juices will run clear.

1 Preheat the oven to 190°C/375°F/Gas Mark 5, 10 minutes before roasting. Heat the oil in a frying pan and gently cook the onion for 5 minutes. Stir in the garlic, celery and chilli and continue to cook for 3–4 minutes.

2 Place the rice and the stock in a large saucepan and cook, covered, for 10–12 minutes or until the rice is tender and all the liquid is absorbed. Stir in the onion and celery mixture, then leave to cool. Once the rice mixture is cold, stir in the chopped mint and season to taste with salt and pepper.

3 Place the boned lamb skin-side down and spoon the rice mixture along the centre of the meat. Roll up the meat to enclose the stuffing and tie securely with string. Weigh the lamb after stuffing and allow it to come to room temperature before roasting. For medium-cooked lamb, allow 25 minutes per 450 g/ 1 lb plus 25 minutes; for well-done, allow 30 minutes per 450 g/1 lb plus 30 minutes. Place in a roasting tin and roast in the preheated oven until cooked to personal preference. Remove from the oven and leave to rest in a warm place for 20 minutes, before carving. Serve with a selection of cooked vegetables.

1

2

3

Potato & Goats' Cheese Tart

INGREDIENTS

Serves 6

275 g/10 oz prepared shortcrust
  pastry, thawed if frozen
550 g/1¼ lb small waxy potatoes
salt and freshly ground black pepper
beaten egg, for brushing
2 tbsp sun-dried tomato paste
¼ tsp chilli powder, or to taste
1 large egg
150 ml/¼ pint soured cream
150 ml/¼ pint milk
2 tbsp freshly snipped chives
300 g/11 oz goats' cheese, sliced
salad and warm crusty bread,
  to serve

HELPFUL HINT

Using ready-made shortcrust pastry is a good way to save time, but always remove it from the refrigerator 10–15 minutes before rolling out, otherwise it may be difficult to handle. Brushing the base with egg helps seal the pastry and keeps it crisp when filled.

1 Preheat the oven to 190°C/375°F/Gas Mark 5, about 10 minutes before cooking. Roll the pastry out on a lightly floured surface and use to line a 23 cm/9 inch fluted flan tin. Chill in the refrigerator for 30 minutes.

2 Scrub the potatoes, place in a large saucepan of lightly salted water and bring to the boil. Simmer for 10–15 minutes, or until the potatoes are tender. Drain and reserve until cool enough to handle.

3 Line the pastry case with greaseproof paper and baking beans or crumpled tinfoil and bake blind in the preheated oven for 15 minutes. Remove from the oven and discard the paper and beans or tinfoil. Brush the base with a little beaten egg, then return to the oven and cook for a further 5 minutes. Remove from the oven.

4 Cut the potatoes into 1 cm/ ½ inch thick slices and reserve. Spread the sun-dried tomato paste over the base of pastry case, sprinkle with the chilli powder, then arrange the potato slices on top in a decorative pattern.

5 Beat together the egg, soured cream, milk and chives, then season to taste with salt and pepper. Pour over the potatoes. Arrange the goats' cheese on top of the potatoes. Bake in the preheated oven for 30 minutes until golden brown and set. Serve immediately with salad and warm bread.

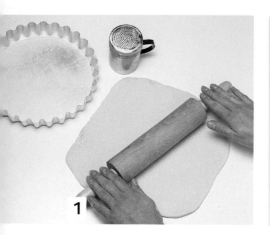

1

3

4

Wild Mushroom Risotto

INGREDIENTS

Serves 6

60 g/2 oz dried porcini or morel
   mushrooms
about 500 g/1 lb 2 oz mixed fresh
   wild mushrooms, such as porcini,
   girolles, horse mushrooms and
   chanterelles, cleaned and halved if
   large
4 tbsp olive oil
3–4 garlic cloves, finely chopped
60 g/2 oz unsalted butter
1 onion, finely chopped
350 g/12 oz arborio or carnaroli rice
50 ml/2 fl oz dry white vermouth
1.2 litres/2 pints chicken
   stock, simmering
115 g/4 oz freshly grated
   Parmesan cheese
4 tbsp fresh flat-leaf parsley, chopped
salt and pepper

1 Cover the dried mushrooms with boiling water. Leave to soak for 30 minutes, then carefully lift out and pat dry. Strain the soaking liquid through a sieve lined with a paper towel, and set aside.

2 Trim the wild mushrooms and gently brush clean.

3 Heat 3 tablespoons of the oil in a large frying pan until hot. Add the fresh mushrooms, and stir-fry for 1–2 minutes. Add the garlic and the soaked mushrooms and cook for 2 minutes, stirring frequently. Scrape on to a plate and set aside.

4 Heat the remaining oil and half the butter in a large heavy based saucepan. Add the onion and cook for about 2 minutes until softened. Add the rice and cook, stirring frequently, for about 2 minutes until translucent and well coated.

5 Add the vermouth to the rice. When almost absorbed, add a ladleful (about 225 ml/8 fl oz) of the simmering stock. Cook, stirring constantly, until the liquid is absorbed.

6 Continue adding the stock, about half a ladleful at a time, allowing each addition to be absorbed before adding the next. This should take 20–25 minutes. The risotto should have a creamy consistency and the rice should be tender, but firm to the bite.

7 Add half the dried mushroom soaking liquid to the risotto and stir in the mushrooms. Season with salt and pepper, and add more mushroom liquid if necessary. Remove from the heat; stir in the remaining butter, Parmesan and parsley. Serve immediately.

2

3

4

Vegetables Braised in Olive Oil & Lemon

INGREDIENTS

Serves 4

small strip of pared rind and
  juice of ½ lemon
4 tbsp olive oil
1 bay leaf
large sprig of thyme
150 ml/¼ pint water
4 spring onions, trimmed and
  finely chopped
175 g/6 oz baby button mushrooms
175 g/6 oz broccoli, cut into
  small florets
175 g/6 oz cauliflower, cut into
  small florets
1 medium courgette, sliced on
  the diagonal
2 tbsp freshly snipped chives
salt and freshly ground black pepper
lemon zest, to garnish

TASTY TIP

Serve these vegetables as an accompaniment to roasted or grilled chicken, fish or turkey. Alternatively, toast some crusty bread, rub with a garlic clove and drizzle with a little olive oil and top with a spoonful of vegetables.

1 Put the pared lemon rind and juice into a large saucepan. Add the olive oil, bay leaf, thyme and the water. Bring to the boil. Add the spring onions and mushrooms. Top with the broccoli and cauliflower, trying to add them so that the stalks are submerged in the water and the tops are just above it. Cover and simmer for 3 minutes.

2 Scatter the courgettes on top, so that they are steamed rather than boiled. Cook, covered, for a further 3–4 minutes, until all the vegetables are tender. Using a slotted spoon, transfer the vegetables from the liquid into a warmed serving dish. Increase the heat and boil rapidly for 3–4 minutes, or until the liquid is reduced to about 8 tablespoons. Remove the lemon rind, bay leaf and thyme sprig and discard.

3 Stir the chives into the reduced liquid, season to taste with salt and pepper and pour over the vegetables. Sprinkle with lemon zest and serve immediately.

Spinach Dumplings with Rich Tomato Sauce

INGREDIENTS

Serves 4

For the sauce:

2 tbsp olive oil
1 onion, peeled and chopped
1 garlic clove, peeled and crushed
1 red chilli, deseeded and chopped
150 ml/¼ pint dry white wine
400 g can chopped tomatoes
pared strip of lemon rind

For the dumplings:

450 g/1 lb fresh spinach
50 g/2 oz ricotta cheese
25 g/1 oz fresh white breadcrumbs
25 g/1 oz Parmesan cheese, grated
1 medium egg yolk
¼ tsp freshly grated nutmeg
salt and freshly ground black pepper
5 tbsp plain flour
2 tbsp olive oil, for frying
fresh basil leaves, to garnish
freshly cooked tagliatelle, to serve

1. To make the tomato sauce, heat the olive oil in a large saucepan and fry the onion gently for 5 minutes. Add the garlic and chilli and cook for a further 5 minutes, until softened.

2. Stir in the wine, chopped tomatoes and lemon rind. Bring to the boil, cover and simmer for 20 minutes, then uncover and simmer for 15 minutes, or until the sauce has thickened. Remove the lemon rind and season to taste with salt and pepper.

3. To make the spinach dumplings, wash the spinach thoroughly and remove any tough stalks. Cover and cook in a large saucepan over a low heat with just the water clinging to the leaves. Drain, then squeeze out all the excess water. Finely chop and put in a large bowl.

4. Add the ricotta, breadcrumbs, Parmesan cheese and egg yolk to the spinach. Season with nutmeg and salt and pepper. Mix together and shape into 20 walnut-sized balls.

5. Toss the spinach balls in the flour. Heat the olive oil in a large non-stick frying pan and fry the balls gently for 5–6 minutes, carefully turning occasionally. Garnish with fresh basil leaves and serve immediately with the tomato sauce and tagliatelle.

2

4

5

Hot Grilled Chicory & Pears

INGREDIENTS

Serves 4

50 g/2 oz unblanched almonds,
    roughly chopped
4 small heads of chicory
2 tbsp olive oil
1 tbsp walnut oil
2 firm ripe dessert pears
2 tsp lemon juice
1 tsp freshly chopped oregano
salt and freshly ground black pepper
freshly chopped oregano, to garnish
warmed ciabatta bread, to serve

1 Preheat grill. Spread the chopped almonds in a single layer on the grill pan. Cook under a hot grill for about 3 minutes, moving the almonds around occasionally, until lightly browned. Reserve.

2 Halve the chicory lengthways and cut out the cores. Mix together the olive and walnut oils. Brush about 2 tablespoons all over the chicory.

3 Put the chicory in a grill pan, cut-side up and cook under a hot grill for 2–3 minutes, or until beginning to char. Turn and cook for a further 1–2 minutes, then turn again.

4 Peel, core and thickly slice the pears. Brush with 1 tablespoon of the oils, then place the pears on top of the chicory. Grill for a further 3–4 minutes, or until both the chicory and pears are soft.

5 Transfer the chicory and pears to 4 warmed serving plates. Whisk together the remaining oil, lemon juice and oregano and season to taste with salt and pepper.

6 Drizzle the dressing over the chicory and pears and scatter with the toasted almonds. Garnish with fresh oregano and serve with ciabatta bread.

HELPFUL HINT

If preparing the pears ahead of time for this recipe, dip or brush them with some lemon juice to ensure that they do not discolour before cooking.

1

2

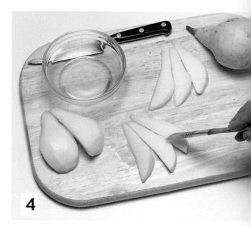
4

Roasted Butternut Squash

INGREDIENTS

Serves 4

2 small butternut squash
4 garlic cloves, peeled
  and crushed
1 tbsp olive oil
salt and freshly ground black pepper
1 tbsp walnut oil
4 medium-sized leeks, trimmed,
  cleaned and thinly sliced
1 tbsp black mustard seeds
300 g can cannellini beans, drained
  and rinsed
125 g/4 oz fine French beans, halved
150 ml/¼ pint vegetable stock
50 g/2 oz rocket
2 tbsp freshly snipped chives
fresh chives, to garnish

To serve:

4 tbsp low-fat fromage frais
mixed salad

1   Preheat the oven to 200°C/400°F/Gas Mark 6. Cut the butternut squash in half lengthways and scoop out all of the seeds.

2   Score the squash in a diamond pattern with a sharp knife. Mix the garlic with the olive oil and brush over the cut surfaces of the squash. Season well with salt and pepper. Put on a baking sheet and roast for 40 minutes until tender.

3   Heat the walnut oil in a saucepan and fry the leeks and mustard seeds for 5 minutes.

4   Add the drained cannellini beans, French beans and vegetable stock. Bring to the boil and simmer gently for 5 minutes until the French beans are tender.

5   Remove from the heat and stir in the rocket and chives. Season well. Remove the squash from the oven and allow to cool for 5 minutes. Spoon in the bean mixture. Garnish with a few snipped chives and serve immediately with the fromage frais and a mixed salad.

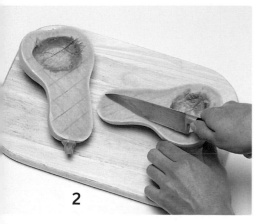

2

3

5

Peperonata

INGREDIENTS

Serves 6

2 red peppers

2 yellow peppers

450 g/1 lb waxy potatoes

1 large onion

2 tbsp good quality virgin olive oil

700 g/1½ lb tomatoes, peeled,
deseeded and chopped

2 small courgettes

50 g/2 oz pitted black
olives, quartered

small handful basil leaves

salt and freshly ground black pepper

crusty bread, to serve

FOOD FACT

This dish is delicious served with Parmesan melba toasts. To make simply remove the crusts from 4 slices of thin white bread. Lightly toast and allow to cool before splitting each piece in half by slicing horizontally. Cut diagonally into triangles, place under a hot grill and toast each side for a few minutes until golden and curling at the edges. Sprinkle with finely grated fresh Parmesan cheese and melt under the grill.

1 Prepare the peppers by halving them lengthways and removing the stems, seeds, and membranes.

2 Cut the peppers lengthways into strips about 1 cm/½ inch wide. Peel the potatoes and cut into rough dice, about 2.5–3 cm/1–1¼ inch across. Cut the onion lengthways into 8 wedges.

3 Heat the olive oil in a large saucepan over a medium heat.

4 Add the onion and cook for about 5 minutes, or until starting to brown.

5 Add the peppers, potatoes, tomatoes, courgettes, black olives and about 4 torn basil leaves. Season to taste with salt and pepper.

6 Stir the mixture, cover and cook over a very low heat for about 40 minutes, or until the vegetables are tender but still hold their shape. Garnish with the remaining basil. Transfer to a serving bowl and serve immediately, with chunks of crusty bread.

1

4

5

Marinated Vegetable Kebabs

INGREDIENTS

Serves 4

2 small courgettes, cut into
  2 cm/^{3}/$_4$ inch pieces
^{1}/$_2$ green pepper, deseeded and cut
  into 2.5 cm/1 inch pieces
^{1}/$_2$ red pepper, deseeded and cut into
  2.5 cm /1 inch pieces
^{1}/$_2$ yellow pepper, deseeded and cut
  into 2.5 cm/1 inch pieces
8 baby onions, peeled
8 button mushrooms
8 cherry tomatoes
freshly chopped parsley,
  to garnish
freshly cooked couscous,
  to serve

For the marinade:

1 tbsp light olive oil
4 tbsp dry sherry
2 tbsp light soy sauce
1 red chilli, deseeded and
  finely chopped
2 garlic cloves, peeled and crushed
2.5 cm/1 inch piece root ginger,
  peeled and finely grated

1 Place the courgettes, peppers and baby onions in a pan of just boiled water. Bring back to the boil and simmer for about 30 seconds.

2 Drain and rinse the cooked vegetables in cold water and dry on absorbent kitchen paper.

3 Thread the cooked vegetables and the mushrooms and tomatoes alternately on to skewers and place in a large shallow dish.

4 Make the marinade by whisking all the ingredients together until thoroughly blended. Pour the marinade evenly over the kebabs, then chill in the refrigerator for at least 1 hour. Spoon the marinade over the kebabs occasionally during this time.

5 Place the kebabs in a hot griddle pan or on a hot barbecue and cook gently for 10–12 minutes. Turn the kebabs frequently and brush with the marinade when needed. When the vegetables are tender, sprinkle over the chopped parsley and serve immediately with couscous.

3

4

5

Stuffed Onions with Pine Nuts

INGREDIENTS

Serves 4

4 medium onions, peeled

2 garlic cloves, peeled
    and crushed

2 tbsp fresh brown breadcrumbs

2 tbsp white breadcrumbs

25 g/1 oz sultanas

25 g/1 oz pine nuts

50 g/2 oz low-fat hard cheese such
    as Edam, grated

2 tbsp freshly chopped parsley

1 medium egg, beaten

salt and freshly ground
    black pepper

salad leaves, to serve

1 Preheat the oven to 200°C/400°F/Gas Mark 6. Bring a pan of water to the boil, add the onions and cook gently for about 15 minutes.

2 Drain well. Allow the onions to cool, then slice each one in half horizontally.

3 Scoop out most of the onion flesh but leave a reasonably firm shell.

4 Chop up 4 tablespoons of the onion flesh and place in a bowl with the crushed garlic, breadcrumbs, sultanas, pine nuts, grated cheese and parsley.

5 Mix the breadcrumb mixture together thoroughly. Bind together with as much of the beaten egg as necessary to make a firm filling. Season to taste with salt and pepper.

6 Pile the mixture back into the onion shells and top with the grated cheese. Place on a oiled baking tray and cook in the preheated oven for 20–30 minutes or until golden brown. Serve immediately with the salad leaves.

FOOD FACT

While this dish is delicious on its own, it also compliments barbecued meat and fish. The onion takes on a mellow, nutty flavour when baked.

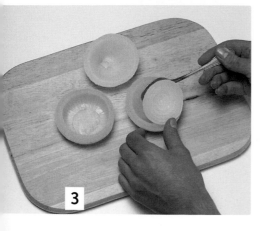

3

4

6

Orange & Fennel Salad

INGREDIENTS

Serves 4

4 large oranges
1 large bulb fennel
2 tsp fennel seeds
2 tbsp extra-virgin olive oil
orange juice, freshly squeezed,
  to taste
fresh parsley, finely chopped,
  to garnish

1   Using a small serrated knife, remove the rind and pith from one orange, cutting carefully from the top to the bottom of the orange so it retains its shape. Work over a bowl to catch the juices.

2   Peel the remaining oranges the same way, reserving all the juices. Cut the oranges horizontally into 5 mm/¼ inch slices and arrange in an attractive serving bowl and reserve the juices.

3   Place the fennel bulb on a chopping board and cut off the fronds. Cut the bulb in half lengthways and then into quarters. Cut crossways into the thinnest slices you can manage. Immediately transfer to the bowl with the oranges and toss with a little of the reserved orange juice to prevent browning.

4   Sprinkle the fennel seeds over the oranges and fennel.

5   Place the olive oil in a small bowl and whisk in the rest of the reserved orange juice, plus extra fresh orange juice to taste. Pour over the oranges and fennel and toss gently. Cover with clingfilm and chill until ready to serve.

6   Just before serving, remove from the refrigerator and sprinkle with parsley. Serve chilled.

2

3

4

Tortellini & Summer Vegetable Salad

INGREDIENTS

Serves 6

350 g/12 oz plain cheese-filled
  fresh tortellini

150 ml/¼ pint extra-virgin olive oil

225 g/8 oz fine green beans, trimmed

175 g/6 oz broccoli florets

1 yellow or red pepper, deseeded and
  thinly sliced

1 red onion, peeled and sliced

175 g jar marinated artichoke hearts,
  drained and halved

2 tbsp capers

75 g/3 oz dry-cured pitted black olives

3 tbsp raspberry or balsamic vinegar

1 tbsp Dijon mustard

1 tsp soft brown sugar

salt and freshly ground black pepper

2 tbsp freshly chopped basil or flat-
  leaf parsley

2 quartered hard-boiled eggs,
  to garnish

1. Bring a large pan of lightly salted water to a rolling boil. Add the tortellini and cook according to the packet instructions, or until 'al dente'.

2. Using a large slotted spoon, transfer the tortellini to a colander to drain. Rinse under cold running water and drain again. Transfer to a large bowl and toss with 2 tablespoons of the olive oil.

3. Return the pasta water to the boil and drop in the green beans and broccoli florets; blanch them for 2 minutes, or until just beginning to soften. Drain, rinse under cold running water and drain again thoroughly. Add the vegetables to the reserved tortellini.

4. Add the pepper, onion, artichoke hearts, capers and olives to the bowl. Stir lightly.

5. Whisk together the vinegar, mustard and brown sugar in a bowl and season to taste with salt and pepper. Slowly whisk in the remaining olive oil to form a thick, creamy dressing. Pour over the tortellini and vegetables, add the chopped basil or parsley and stir until lightly coated. Transfer to a shallow serving dish or salad bowl. Garnish with the hard-boiled egg quarters and serve.

FOOD FACT

Black olives are picked when fully ripe and a brownish pink colour and then fermented and oxidised until they become black.

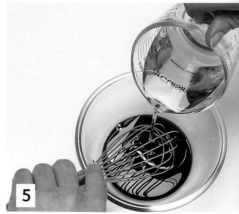

Rice & Papaya Salad

INGREDIENTS

Serves 4

175 g/6 oz easy-cook basmati rice

1 cinnamon stick, bruised

1 bird's-eye chilli, deseeded and
  finely chopped

rind and juice of 2 limes

rind and juice of 2 lemons

2 tbsp Thai fish sauce

1 tbsp soft light brown sugar

1 papaya, peeled and seeds removed

1 mango, peeled and stone removed

1 green chilli, deseeded and
  finely chopped

2 tbsp freshly chopped coriander

1 tbsp freshly chopped mint

250 g/9 oz cooked chicken

50 g/2 oz roasted peanuts, chopped

strips of pitta bread, to serve

1 Rinse and drain the rice and pour into a saucepan. Add 450 ml/ ³/₄ pint boiling salted water and the cinnamon stick. Bring to the boil, reduce the heat to a very low heat, cover and cook without stirring for 15–18 minutes, or until all the liquid is absorbed. The rice should be light and fluffy and have steam holes on the surface. Remove the cinnamon stick and stir in the rind from 1 lime.

2 To make the dressing, place the bird's-eye chilli, remaining rind and lime and lemon juice, fish sauce and sugar in a food processor, mix for a few minutes until blended. Alternatively, place all these ingredients in a screw-top jar and shake until well blended. Pour half the dressing over the hot rice and toss until the rice glistens.

3 Slice the papaya and mango into thin slices, then place in a bowl. Add the chopped green chilli, coriander and mint. Place the chicken on a chopping board, then remove and discard any skin or sinews. Cut into fine shreds and add to the bowl with the chopped peanuts.

4 Add the remaining dressing to the chicken mixture and stir until all the ingredients are lightly coated. Spoon the rice onto a platter, pile the chicken mixture on top and serve with warm strips of pitta bread.

HELPFUL HINT

The papaya or pawpaw's skin turns from green when unripe, through to yellow and orange. To prepare, cut in half lengthways, scoop out the black seeds with a teaspoon and discard. Cut away the thin skin before slicing.

2

3

3

Bulghur Wheat Salad with Minty Lemon Dressing

INGREDIENTS

Serves 4

125 g/4 oz bulghur wheat
10 cm /4 inch piece cucumber
2 shallots, peeled
125 g/4 oz baby sweetcorn
3 ripe but firm tomatoes

For the dressing:

grated rind of 1 lemon
3 tbsp lemon juice
3 tbsp freshly chopped mint
2 tbsp freshly chopped parsley
1–2 tsp clear honey
2 tbsp sunflower oil
salt and freshly ground
   black pepper

1 Place the bulghur wheat in a saucepan and cover with boiling water.

2 Simmer for about 10 minutes, then drain thoroughly and turn into a serving bowl.

3 Cut the cucumber into small dice, chop the shallots finely and reserve. Steam the sweetcorn over a pan of boiling water for 10 minutes or until tender. Drain and slice into thick chunks.

4 Cut a cross on the top of each tomato and place in boiling water until their skins start to peel away.

5 Remove the skins and the seeds and cut the tomatoes into small dice.

6 Make the dressing by briskly whisking all the ingredients in a small bowl until mixed well.

7 When the bulghur wheat has cooled a little, add all the prepared vegetables and stir in the dressing. Season to taste with salt and pepper and serve.

FOOD FACT

This dish is loosely based on the Middle Eastern dish tabbouleh, a type of salad in which all the ingredients are mixed together and served cold.

2

3

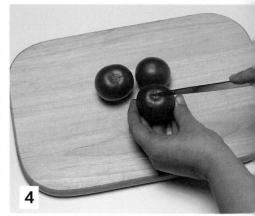

4

Warm Fruity Rice Salad

INGREDIENTS

Serves 4

175 g/6 oz mixed basmati and
  wild rice
125 g/4 oz skinless chicken breast
300 ml/½ pint chicken or
  vegetable stock
125 g/4 oz ready-to-eat
  dried apricots
125 g/4 oz ready-to-eat
  dried dates
3 sticks celery

For the dressing:

2 tbsp sunflower oil
1 tbsp white wine vinegar
4 tbsp lemon juice
1–2 tsp clear honey, warmed
1 tsp Dijon mustard
freshly ground black pepper

To garnish:

6 spring onions
sprigs of fresh coriander

1. Place the rice in a pan of boiling salted water and cook for 15–20 minutes or until tender. Rinse thoroughly with boiling water and reserve.

2. Meanwhile wipe the chicken and place in a shallow saucepan with the stock.

3. Bring to the boil, cover and simmer for about 15 minutes or until the chicken is cooked thoroughly and the juices run clear.

4. Leave the chicken in the stock until cool enough to handle, then cut into thin slices.

5. Chop the apricots and dates into small pieces. Peel any tough membranes from the outside of the celery and chop into dice. Fold the apricots, dates, celery and sliced chicken into the warm rice.

6. Make the dressing by whisking all the ingredients together in a small bowl until mixed thoroughly. Pour 2–3 tablespoons over the rice and stir in gently and evenly. Serve the remaining dressing separately.

7. Trim and chop the spring onions. Sprinkle the spring onions over the top of the salad and garnish with the sprigs of coriander. Serve while still warm.

2

5

6

Warm Leek & Tomato Salad

INGREDIENTS

Serves 4

450 g/1 lb trimmed baby leeks
225 g/8 oz ripe, but firm tomatoes
2 shallots, peeled and cut into
thin wedges

For the honey and lime dressing:

2 tbsp clear honey
grated rind of 1 lime
4 tbsp lime juice
1 tbsp light olive oil
1 tsp Dijon mustard
salt and freshly ground
black pepper

To garnish:

freshly chopped tarragon
freshly chopped basil

1 Trim the leeks so that they are all the same length. Place in a steamer over a pan of boiling water and steam for 8 minutes or until just tender.

2 Drain the leeks thoroughly and arrange in a shallow serving dish.

3 Make a cross in the top of the tomatoes, place in a bowl and cover them with boiling water until their skins start to peel away. Remove from the bowl and carefully remove the skins.

4 Cut the tomatoes into 4 and remove the seeds, then chop into small dice. Spoon over the top of the leeks together with the shallots.

5 In a small bowl make the dressing by whisking the honey, lime rind, lime juice, olive oil, mustard and salt and pepper. Pour 3 tablespoons of the dressing over the leeks and tomatoes and garnish with the tarragon and basil. Serve while the leeks are still warm, with the remaining dressing served separately.

HELPFUL HINT

An easy way to measure honey is to plunge a metal measuring spoon into boiling water. Drain the spoon, then dip into the honey.

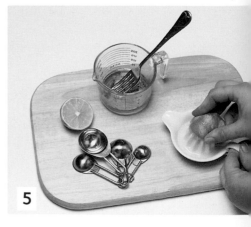

Mediterranean Rice Salad

INGREDIENTS

Serves 4

250 g/9 oz Camargue red rice
2 sun-dried tomatoes, finely chopped
2 garlic cloves, peeled and
   finely chopped
4 tbsp oil from a jar of sun-
   dried tomatoes
2 tsp balsamic vinegar
2 tsp red wine vinegar
salt and freshly ground black pepper
1 red onion, peeled and thinly sliced
1 yellow pepper, quartered
   and deseeded
1 red pepper, quartered and deseeded
½ cucumber, peeled and diced
6 ripe plum tomatoes, cut
   into wedges
1 fennel bulb, halved and thinly sliced
fresh basil leaves, to garnish

FOOD FACT

Camargue red rice from the south of France is a reddish-brown colour and gives this salad a stunning appearance. It has a texture and cooking time similar to that of brown rice, which may be substituted in this recipe if Camargue red rice is unavailable.

1 Cook the rice in a saucepan of lightly salted boiling water for 35–40 minutes, or until tender. Drain well and reserve.

2 Whisk the sun-dried tomatoes, garlic, oil and vinegars together in a small bowl or jug. Season to taste with salt and pepper. Put the red onion in a large bowl, pour over the dressing and leave to allow the flavours to develop.

3 Put the peppers, skin-side up on a grill rack and cook under a preheated hot grill for 5–6 minutes, or until blackened and charred. Remove and place in a plastic bag. When cool enough to handle, peel off the skins and slice the peppers.

4 Add the peppers, cucumber, tomatoes, fennel and rice to the onions. Mix gently together to coat in the dressing. Cover and chill in the refrigerator for 30 minutes to allow the flavours to mingle.

5 Remove the salad from the refrigerator and leave to stand at room temperature for 20 minutes. Garnish with fresh basil leaves and serve.

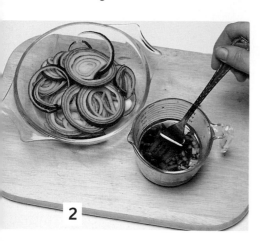

2

3

4

Winter Coleslaw

INGREDIENTS

Serves 6

175 g/6 oz white cabbage
1 medium red onion, peeled
175 g/6 oz carrot, peeled
175 g/6 oz celeriac, peeled
2 celery stalks, trimmed
75 g/3 oz golden sultanas

For the yogurt & herb dressing:
150 ml/¼ pint low-fat
   natural yogurt
1 garlic clove, peeled
   and crushed
1 tbsp lemon juice
1 tsp clear honey
1 tbsp freshly snipped chives

TASTY TIP
To make cheese coleslaw, simply replace the sultanas with 75 g/ 3 oz of reduced-fat cheese. Whether the winter or cheese variety, coleslaw is particularly good with baked potatoes and a little low-fat spread.

1. Remove the hard core from the cabbage with a small knife and shred finely.

2. Slice the onion finely and coarsely grate the carrot.

3. Place the raw vegetables in a large bowl and mix together.

4. Cut the celeriac into thin strips and simmer in boiling water for about 2 minutes.

5. Drain the celeriac and rinse thoroughly with cold water.

6. Chop the celery and add to the bowl with the celeriac and sultanas and mix well.

7. Make the yogurt and herb dressing by briskly whisking the yogurt, garlic, lemon juice, honey and chives together.

8. Pour the dressing over the top of the salad. Stir the vegetables thoroughly to coat evenly and serve.

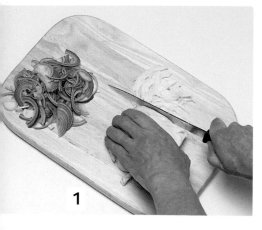

1

4

6

Warm Potato, Pear & Pecan Salad

INGREDIENTS

Serves 4

900 g/2 lb new potatoes, preferably
  red-skinned, unpeeled
salt and freshly ground black pepper
1 tsp Dijon mustard
2 tsp white wine vinegar
3 tbsp groundnut oil
1 tbsp hazelnut or walnut oil
2 tsp poppy seeds
2 firm ripe dessert pears
2 tsp lemon juice
175 g/6 oz baby spinach leaves
75 g/3 oz toasted pecan nuts

HELPFUL HINT

To toast the pecan nuts, place on a baking tray in a single layer and cook in a preheated oven at 180°C/350°F/Gas Mark 4 for 5 minutes, or under a medium grill for 3–4 minutes, turning frequently. Watch them carefully – they burn easily. If you can not get red-skinned new potatoes for this dish, add colour by using red-skinned pears instead. Look out for Red Bartlett and Red Williams.

1 Scrub the potatoes, then cook in a saucepan of lightly salted boiling water for 15 minutes, or until tender. Drain, cut into halves, or quarters if large, and place in a serving bowl.

2 In a small bowl or jug, whisk together the mustard and vinegar. Gradually add the oils until the mixture begins to thicken. Stir in the poppy seeds and season to taste with salt and pepper.

3 Pour about two-thirds of the dressing over the hot potatoes and toss gently to coat. Leave until the potatoes have soaked up the dressing and are just warm.

4 Meanwhile, quarter and core the pears. Cut into thin slices, then sprinkle with the lemon juice to prevent them from going brown. Add to the potatoes with the spinach leaves and toasted pecan nuts. Gently mix together.

5 Drizzle the remaining dressing over the salad. Serve immediately before the spinach starts to wilt.

1

2

4

Squid Salad

INGREDIENTS

Serves 4

900 g/2 lb small squid
120 ml/4 fl oz lemon juice
60 ml/2 fl oz extra-virgin olive oil
25 g/1 oz fresh flat-leaf parsley
8 spring onions
4 vine-ripened tomatoes, deseeded
  and chopped
salt and pepper

To garnish:

radicchio leaves
red chillies, finely chopped (optional)
capers or black olives (optional)
fresh flat-leaf parsley, finely chopped

1 To prepare each squid, pull the head and all the insides out of the body sac. Cut the tentacles off the head and discard the head. Remove the beak from the centre of the tentacles.

2 Pull out the thin, transparent quill that runs through the centre of the body. Rinse the body sac under running cold water and, using your fingers, rub off the thin, grey membrane. Cut the squid body sacs into 1 cm/½ inch slices. Rinse the tentacle pieces and set aside with the body slices.

3 Put the lemon juice and olive oil in a large bowl and stir together. Very finely chop the parsley and add to the bowl. Finely chop the white parts of the spring onions and add to the bowl with the tomatoes. Season with salt and pepper to taste.

4 Bring a pan of lightly salted water to the boil. Add all the squid and return to the boil.

5 As soon as the water returns to the boil, drain the squid. Add the squid to the bowl of dressing and gently toss all the ingredients together.

6 Leave the squid to cool completely, then cover and leave to marinate in the refrigerator for at least 6 hours, preferably overnight.

7 Line a serving bowl with radicchio leaves. Add the chopped chilli, capers or olives, to taste, if using. Mound the squid salad on top of the radicchio leaves and sprinkle with finely chopped parsley. Serve very chilled.

1

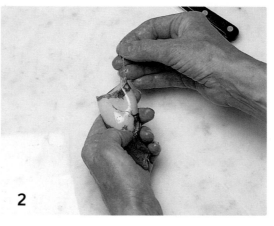

2

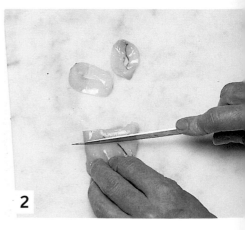

2

Lobster Salad

INGREDIENTS

Serves 2

2 raw lobster tails
salt and pepper

For the lemon-dill mayonnaise:

1 large lemon
1 large egg yolk
½ tsp Dijon mustard
150 ml/5 fl oz olive oil
1 tbsp fresh dill, chopped

To garnish:

radicchio leaves
lemon wedges
fresh dill sprigs

1   To make the lemon-dill mayonnaise, finely grate the rind from the lemon and squeeze the juice. Beat the egg yolk in a small bowl and beat in the mustard and 1 teaspoon of the lemon juice.

2   Using a balloon whisk or electric mixer, beat in the olive oil, drop by drop, until a thick mayonnaise forms. Stir in half the lemon rind and 1 tablespoon of the juice.

3   Season with salt and pepper, and add more lemon juice if desired. Stir in the dill and cover with clingfilm. Chill until required.

4   Bring a large saucepan of salted water to the boil. Add the lobster tails and continue to cook for 6 minutes until the flesh is opaque and the shells are red. Drain immediately and leave to cool completely.

5   Remove the lobster flesh from the shells and cut into bite-sized pieces. Arrange the radicchio leaves on individual plates and top with the lobster flesh. Place a spoonful of the lemon-dill mayonnaise on the side. Garnish with lemon wedges and dill sprigs and serve.

4

4

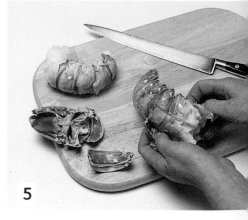

5

Tuna Bean Salad

INGREDIENTS

Serves 4

225 g/8 oz dried haricot beans
1 tbsp lemon juice
5 tbsp extra-virgin olive oil, plus
    extra for brushing
1 garlic clove, finely chopped
1 small red onion, very finely
    sliced (optional)
1 tbsp chopped fresh parsley
4 x 175 g/6 oz tuna steaks
salt and pepper

To Garnish:

parsley sprigs
lemon wedges

1 Soak the haricot beans for 8 hours or overnight in at least twice their volume of cold water.

2 When you are ready to cook, drain the beans and place in a saucepan with twice their volume of fresh water. Bring slowly to the boil, skimming off any scum that rises to the surface. Boil the beans rapidly for 10 minutes, then reduce the heat and simmer for a further $1\frac{1}{4}$–$1\frac{1}{2}$ hours until the beans are tender.

3 Meanwhile, mix together the lemon juice, olive oil, garlic and seasoning. Drain the beans thoroughly and mix together with the olive oil mixture, onion and parsley. Season to taste and set aside.

4 Wash and dry the tuna steaks. Brush lightly with olive oil and season. Cook on a preheated ridged grill pan for 2 minutes on each side until just pink in the centre.

5 Divide the bean salad between 4 serving plates. Top each with a tuna steak. Garnish with parsley sprigs and lemon wedges and serve immediately.

1

4

5

Mixed Salad with Anchovy Dressing & Ciabatta Croûtons

INGREDIENTS

Serves 4

1 small head endive
1 small head chicory
1 fennel bulb
400 g can artichokes, drained
  and rinsed
½ cucumber
125 g/4 oz cherry tomatoes
75 g/3 oz black olives

For the anchovy dressing:

50 g can anchovy fillets
1 tsp Dijon mustard
1 small garlic clove, peeled
  and crushed
4 tbsp olive oil
1 tbsp lemon juice
freshly ground black pepper

For the ciabatta croûtons:

2 thick slices ciabatta bread
2 tbsp olive oil

1 Divide the endive and chicory into leaves and reserve some of the larger ones. Arrange the smaller leaves in a wide salad bowl.

2 Cut the fennel bulb in half from the stalk to the root end, then cut across in fine slices. Quarter the artichokes, then quarter and slice the cucumber and halve the tomatoes. Add to the salad bowl with the olives.

3 To make the dressing, drain the anchovies and put in a blender with the mustard, garlic, olive oil, lemon juice, 2 tablespoons of hot water and black pepper. Whizz together until smooth and thickened.

4 To make the croûtons, cut the bread into 1 cm/½ inch cubes. Heat the oil in a frying pan, add the bread cubes and fry for 3 minutes, turning frequently until golden. Remove and drain on absorbent kitchen paper.

5 Drizzle half the anchovy dressing over the prepared salad and toss to coat. Arrange the reserved endive and chicory leaves around the edge, then drizzle over the remaining dressing. Scatter over the croûtons and serve immediately.

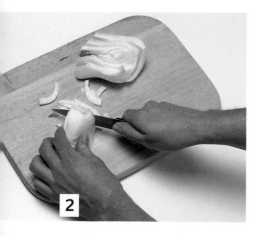

2

3

4

Seared Scallop Salad

INGREDIENTS

Serves 4

12 king (large) scallops
1 tbsp low-fat spread or butter
2 tbsp orange juice
2 tbsp balsamic vinegar
1 tbsp clear honey
2 ripe pears, washed
125 g/4 oz rocket
125 g/4 oz watercress
50 g/2 oz walnuts
freshly ground black pepper

FOOD FACT

As well as the king scallops which are used in this recipe, there are also the smaller queen scallops. It is worth noting that scallops are in season between September and March, when they will not only be at their best, but they may also be slightly cheaper in price. When buying, especially the larger king scallop, make sure that the orange roe is left intact.

1 Clean the scallops removing the thin black vein from around the white meat and coral. Rinse thoroughly and dry on absorbent kitchen paper.

2 Cut into 2–3 thick slices, depending on the scallop size.

3 Heat a griddle pan or heavy-based frying pan, then when hot, add the low-fat spread or butter and allow to melt.

4 Once melted, sear the scallops for 1 minute on each side or until golden. Remove from the pan and reserve.

5 Briskly whisk together the orange juice, balsamic vinegar and honey to make the dressing and reserve.

6 With a small sharp knife carefully cut the pears into quarters, core then cut into chunks.

7 Mix the rocket leaves, watercress, pear chunks and walnuts. Pile on to serving plates and top with the scallops.

8 Drizzle over the dressing and grind over plenty of black pepper. Serve immediately.

1

4

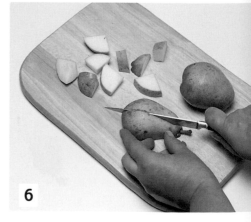

6

Curly Endive & Seafood Salad

INGREDIENTS

Serves 4

1 head of curly endive lettuce
2 green peppers
12.5 cm/5 inch piece cucumber
125 g/4 oz squid, cleaned and cut
  into thin rings
225 g/8 oz baby asparagus spears
125 g/4 oz smoked salmon slices,
  cut into wide strips
175 g/6 oz fresh cooked mussels
  in their shells

For the lemon Dressing:

2 tbsp sunflower oil
1 tbsp white wine vinegar
5 tbsp fresh lemon juice
1–2 tsp caster sugar
1 tsp mild whole-grain mustard
salt and freshly ground
  black pepper

To garnish:

slices of lemon
sprigs of fresh coriander

1 Rinse and tear the endive into small pieces and arrange on a serving platter.

2 Remove the seeds from the peppers and cut the peppers and the cucumber into small dice. Sprinkle over the endive.

3 Bring a saucepan of water to the boil and add the squid rings. Bring the pan up to the boil again, then switch off the heat and leave it to stand for 5 minutes. Then drain and rinse thoroughly in cold water.

4 Cook the asparagus in boiling water for 5 minutes or until tender but just crisp. Arrange with the squid, smoked salmon and mussels on top of the salad.

5 To make the lemon dressing, put all the ingredients into a screw-topped jar or into a small bowl and mix thoroughly until the ingredients are combined.

6 Spoon 3 tablespoons of the dressing over the salad and serve the remainder in a small jug. Garnish the salad with slices of lemon and sprigs of coriander and serve.

2

3

4

Coffee & Peach Creams

INGREDIENTS

Serves 4

4 peaches
50 g/2 oz caster sugar
2 tbsp coffee essence
200 g carton half-fat Greek
 set yogurt
300 g carton half-fat
 ready-made custard

To decorate:

peach slices
sprigs of mint
low-fat crème fraîche

1 Cut the peaches in half and remove the stones. Place the peaches in a large bowl, cover with boiling water and leave for 2–3 minutes.

2 Drain the peaches, then carefully remove the skin.

3 Place the caster sugar in a saucepan and add 50 ml/2 fl oz water.

4 Bring the sugar mixture to the boil, stirring occasionally, until the sugar has dissolved. Boil rapidly for about 2 minutes.

5 Add the peaches and coffee essence to the pan. Remove from the heat and allow the peach mixture to cool.

6 Meanwhile mix together the Greek yogurt and custard until well combined.

7 Divide the peaches between the 4 glass dishes.

8 Spoon over the custard mixture then top with remaining peach mixture.

9 Chill for 30 minutes and then serve, decorated with peach slices, mint sprigs and a little crème fraîche.

FOOD FACT

It is generally believed that peaches originated from China. There are over 2,000 varieties grown throughout the world.

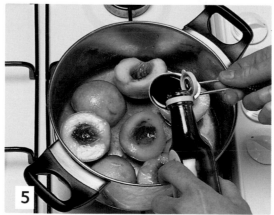

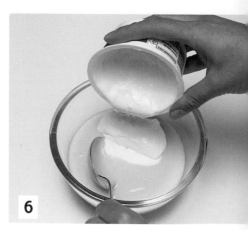

Poached Pears

INGREDIENTS

Serves 4

2 small cinnamon sticks
125 g/4 oz caster sugar
300 ml/½ pint red wine
150 ml/¼ pint water
thinly pared rind and juice of
 1 small orange
4 firm pears
orange slices, to decorate
frozen vanilla yogurt, or
 low-fat ice cream, to serve

TASTY TIP

Poached pears are delicious served with a little half-fat crème fraîche and sprinkled with toasted almonds. To toast almonds, simply warm the grill and place whole, blanched almonds or flaked almonds on to a piece of tinfoil. Place under the grill and toast lightly on both sides for 1–2 minutes until golden. Remove and cool, chop if liked.

1 Place the cinnamon sticks on the work surface and with a rolling pin, slowly roll down the side of the cinnamon stick to bruise. Place in a large heavy-based saucepan.

2 Add the sugar, wine, water, pared orange rind and juice to the pan and bring slowly to the boil, stirring occasionally, until the sugar is dissolved.

3 Meanwhile peel the pears, leaving the stalks on.

4 Cut out the cores from the bottom of the pears and level them so that they stand upright.

5 Stand the pears in the syrup, cover the pan and simmer for 20 minutes or until tender.

6 Remove the pan from the heat and leave the pears to cool in the syrup, turning occasionally.

7 Arrange the pears on serving plates and spoon over the syrup. Decorate with the orange slices and serve with the yogurt or low-fat ice cream and any remaining juices.

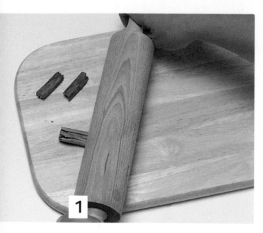

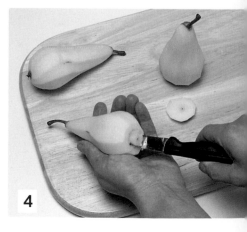

Caramelised Oranges in an Iced Bowl

INGREDIENTS

Serves 4

8 medium-sized oranges
225 g/8 oz caster sugar
4 tbsp Grand Marnier or Cointreau

For the ice bowl:
about 36 ice cubes
fresh flowers and fruits

1 Set freezer to rapid freeze. Place a few ice cubes in the base of a 1.7 litre/3 pint freezable glass bowl. Place a 900 ml /1½ pint glass bowl on top of the ice cubes. Arrange the flower heads and fruits in between the 2 bowls, wedging in position with the ice cubes.

2 Weigh down the smaller bowl with some heavy weights, then carefully pour cold water between the 2 bowls making sure that the flowers and the fruit are covered. Freeze for at least 6 hours or until the ice is frozen solid.

3 When ready to use, remove the weights and using a hot damp cloth rub the inside of the smaller bowl with the cloth until it loosens sufficiently for you to remove the bowl. Place the larger bowl in the sink or washing-up bowl, half filled with very hot water. Leave for about 30 seconds or until the ice loosens. Take care not to leave the bowl in the water for too long otherwise the ice will melt. Remove the bowl and leave in the refrigerator. Return the freezer to its normal setting.

4 Thinly pare the rind from 2 oranges and then cut into julienne strips. Using a sharp knife cut away the rind and pith from all the oranges, holding over a bowl to catch the juices. Slice the oranges, discarding any pips and reform each orange back to its original shape. Secure with cocktail sticks, then place in a bowl.

5 Heat 300 ml/½ pint water, orange rind and sugar together in a pan. Stir the sugar until dissolved. Bring to the boil. Boil for 15 minutes, until it is a caramel colour. Remove pan from heat.

HELPFUL HINT

This iced bowl can hold any dessert. Why not fill with flavoured ice creams?

6 Stir in the liqueur, pour over the oranges. Allow to cool. Chill for 3 hours, turning the oranges occasionally. Spoon into the ice bowl and serve.

Raspberry Sorbet Crush

INGREDIENTS

Serves 4

225 g/8 oz raspberries, thawed
 if frozen
grated rind and juice of 1 lime
300 ml/½ pint orange juice
225 g/8 oz caster sugar
2 medium egg whites

1 Set the freezer to rapid freeze. If using fresh raspberries pick over and lightly rinse.

2 Place the raspberries in a dish and, using a masher, mash to a chunky purée.

3 Place the lime rind and juice, orange juice and half the caster sugar in a large heavy-based saucepan.

4 Heat gently stirring frequently until the sugar is dissolved. Bring to the boil and boil rapidly for about 5 minutes.

5 Remove the pan from the heat and pour carefully into a freezable container.

6 Leave to cool, then place in the freezer and freeze for 2 hours, stirring occasionally to break up the ice crystals.

7 Fold the ice mixture into the raspberry purée with a metal spoon and freeze for a further 2 hours, stirring occasionally.

8 Whisk the egg whites until stiff. Then gradually whisk in the remaining caster sugar a tablespoon at a time until the egg white mixture is stiff and glossy.

9 Fold into the raspberry sorbet with a metal spoon and freeze for 1 hour. Spoon into tall glasses and serve immediately. Remember to return the freezer to its normal setting.

FOOD FACT

This recipe contains raw egg and should not be given to babies, young children, pregnant women, the sick, the elderly and those suffering from a recurring illness.

2

7

9

Raspberry Soufflé

INGREDIENTS

Serves 4

125 g/4 oz redcurrants
50 g/2 oz caster sugar
1 sachet (3 tsp) powdered gelatine
3 medium eggs, separated
300 g/¹/₂ pint half-fat Greek yogurt
450 g/1 lb raspberries, thawed
  if frozen

To decorate:

mint sprigs
extra fruits

1 Wrap a band of double-thickness greaseproof paper around four ramekin dishes, making sure that 5 cm/2 inches of the paper stays above the top of each dish. Secure the paper to the dish with an elastic band or Sellotape.

2 Place the redcurrants and 1 tablespoon of the sugar in a small saucepan. Cook for 5 minutes until softened. Remove from the heat, sieve and reserve.

3 Place 3 tablespoons of water in a small bowl and sprinkle over the gelatine. Allow to stand for 5 minutes until spongy. Place the bowl over a pan of simmering water and leave until dissolved. Remove and allow to cool.

4 Beat together the remaining sugar and egg yolks until pale thick and creamy, then fold in the yogurt with a metal spoon or rubber spatula until well blended.

5 Sieve the raspberries and fold into the yogurt mixture with the gelatine. Whisk the egg whites until stiff and fold into the yogurt mixture. Pour into the prepared dishes and chill in the refrigerator for 2 hours until firm.

6 Remove the paper from the dishes and spread the redcurrant purée over the top of the soufflés. Decorate with mint sprigs and extra fruits and serve.

HELPFUL HINT

Soufflés rely on air, so it is important that the egg whites in this recipe are beaten until very stiff in order to support the mixture.

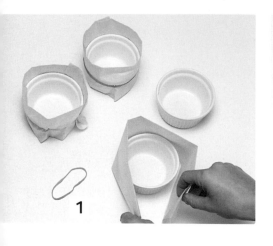

1

3

5

Fruity Roulade

INGREDIENTS

Serves 4

For the sponge:

3 medium eggs
75 g/3 oz caster sugar
75 g/3 oz plain flour, sieved
1–2 tbsp caster sugar for sprinkling

For the filling:

125 g/4 oz Quark
125 g/4 oz half-fat Greek yogurt
25 g/1 oz caster sugar
1 tbsp orange liqueur (optional)
grated rind of 1 orange
125 g/4 oz strawberries, hulled and
   cut into quarters

To decorate:

strawberries
sifted icing sugar

FOOD FACT

Quark is a soft unripened cheese with the flavour and texture of soured cream. It comes in 2 varieties, low fat and non-fat. Quark can be used as a sour cream substitute to top baked potatoes, or in dips and cheesecakes.

1 Preheat the oven to 220°C/425°F/Gas Mark 7. Lightly oil and line a 33 x 23 cm/13 x 9 inch Swiss roll tin with greaseproof or baking parchment paper.

2 Using an electric whisk, whisk the eggs and sugar until the mixture doubles in volume and leaves a trail across the top.

3 Fold in the flour with a metal spoon or rubber spatula. Pour into the prepared tin and bake in the preheated oven for 10–12 minutes, until well risen and golden.

4 Place a whole sheet of greaseproof or baking parchment paper out on a flat work surface and sprinkle evenly with caster sugar.

5 Turn the cooked sponge out on to the paper, discard the paper the sponge was baked on, trim the sponge and roll up encasing the paper inside. Reserve until cool.

6 To make the filling, mix together the Quark, yogurt, caster sugar, liqueur (if using) and orange rind. Unroll the roulade and spread over the mixture. Scatter over the strawberries and roll up.

7 Decorate the roulade with the strawberries. Dust with the icing sugar and serve.

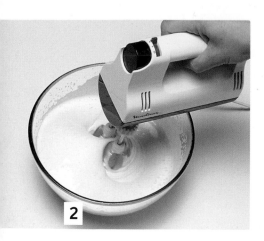

2

5

6

Chocolate Pear Pudding

INGREDIENTS

Serves 6

140 g/4½ oz butter, softened

2 tbsp soft brown sugar

400 g can of pear halves, drained and
 juice reserved

25 g/1 oz walnut halves

125 g/4 oz golden caster sugar

2 medium eggs, beaten

75 g/3 oz self-raising flour, sifted

50 g/2 oz cocoa powder

1 tsp baking powder

prepared chocolate custard, to serve

HELPFUL HINT

To soften butter or margarine quickly, pour hot water in a mixing bowl to warm, leave for a few minutes, then drain and dry. Cut the butter or margarine into small pieces and leave at room temperature for a short time. Do not attempt to melt in the microwave as this will make the fat oily and affect the texture of the finished cake.

1 Preheat the oven to 190°C/375°F/Gas Mark 5, 10 minutes before baking. Butter a 20.5 cm/8 inch sandwich tin with 15 g/½ oz of the butter and sprinkle the base with the soft brown sugar. Arrange the drained pear halves on top of the sugar, cut-side down. Fill the spaces between the pears with the walnut halves, flat-side upwards.

2 Cream the remaining butter with the caster sugar then gradually beat in the beaten eggs, adding 1 tablespoon of the flour after each addition. When all the eggs have been added, stir in the remaining flour.

3 Sift the cocoa powder and baking powder together, then stir into the creamed mixture with 1–2 tablespoons of the reserved pear juice to give a smooth dropping consistency.

4 Spoon the mixture over the pear halves, smoothing the surface. Bake in the preheated oven for 20–25 minutes, or until well risen and the surface springs back when lightly pressed.

5 Remove from the oven and leave to cool for 5 minutes. Using a palate knife, loosen the sides and invert onto a serving plate. Serve with custard.

1

2

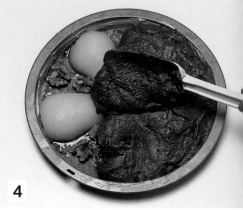

4

Spicy White Chocolate Mousse

INGREDIENTS

Serves 4–6

6 cardamom pods
125 ml/4 fl oz milk
3 bay leaves
200 g/7 oz white chocolate
300 ml/½ pint double cream
3 medium egg whites
1–2 tsp cocoa powder, sifted,
   for dusting

1. Tap the cardamom pods lightly so they split. Remove the seeds, then, using a pestle and mortar, crush lightly. Pour the milk into a small saucepan and add the crushed seeds and the bay leaves. Bring to the boil gently over a medium heat. Remove from the heat, cover and leave in a warm place for at least 30 minutes to infuse.

2. Break the chocolate into small pieces and place in a heatproof bowl set over a saucepan of gently simmering water. Ensure the water is not touching the base of the bowl. When the chocolate has melted remove the bowl from the heat and stir until smooth.

3. Whip the cream until it has slightly thickened and holds its shape, but does not form peaks. Reserve. Whisk the egg whites in a clean, grease-free bowl until stiff and standing in soft peaks.

4. Strain the milk through a sieve into the cooled, melted chocolate and beat until smooth. Spoon the chocolate mixture into the egg whites, then using a large metal spoon, fold gently. Add the whipped cream and fold in gently.

5. Spoon into a large serving dish or individual small cups. Chill in the refrigerator for 3–4 hours. Just before serving, dust with a little sifted cocoa powder and then serve.

TASTY TIP

Chocolate and spices go together very well as this recipe demonstrates. White chocolate has an affinity with spices such as cardamom, while dark and milk chocolate go very well with cinnamon.

2

3

4

White Chocolate Trifle

INGREDIENTS

Serves 6

1 homemade or bought chocolate
  Swiss roll, sliced
4 tbsp brandy
2 tbsp Irish cream liqueur
425 g can black cherries, drained
  and pitted, with 3 tbsp of the
  juice reserved
900 ml/1½ pints double cream
125 g/4 oz white chocolate, broken
  into pieces
6 medium egg yolks
50 g/2 oz caster sugar
2 tsp cornflour
1 tsp vanilla essence
50 g/2 oz plain dark chocolate, grated
50 g/2 oz milk chocolate, grated

HELPFUL HINT

It is critical that the custard is not allowed to boil once the eggs have been added. Otherwise, the mixture turns to sweet scrambled eggs and is unusable. Cook over a very gentle heat, stirring constantly and testing the mixture often.

1 Place the Swiss roll slices in the bottom of a trifle dish and pour over the brandy, Irish cream liqueur and a little of the reserved black cherry juice to moisten the Swiss roll. Arrange the black cherries on the top.

2 Pour 600 ml/1 pint of the cream into a saucepan and add the white chocolate. Heat gently to just below simmering point. Whisk together the egg yolks, caster sugar, cornflour and vanilla essence in a small bowl.

3 Gradually whisk the egg mixture into the hot cream, then strain into a clean saucepan and return to the heat.

4 Cook the custard gently, stirring throughout until thick and coats the back of a spoon.

5 Leave the custard to cool slightly, then pour over the trifle. Leave the trifle to chill in the refrigerator for at least 3–4 hours, or preferably overnight.

6 Before serving, lightly whip the remaining cream until soft peaks form, then spoon the cream over the set custard. Using the back of a spoon, swirl the cream in a decorative pattern. Sprinkle with grated plain and milk chocolate and serve.

2

3

5

White Chocolate Eclairs

INGREDIENTS

Serves 4–6

50 g/2 oz unsalted butter

60 g/2½ oz plain flour, sifted

2 medium eggs, lightly beaten

6 ripe passion fruit

300 ml/½ pint double cream

3 tbsp kirsch

1 tbsp icing sugar

125 g/4 oz white chocolate, broken
  into pieces

HELPFUL HINT

Passion fruit are readily available in supermarkets. They are small, round purplish fruits that should have quite wrinkled skins. Smooth passion fruit are not ripe and will have little juice or flavour.

1 Preheat the oven to 190°C/375°F/Gas Mark 5, 10 minutes before baking. Lightly oil a baking sheet. Place the butter and 150 ml/¼ pint of water in a saucepan and gradually bring to the boil.

2 Remove the saucepan from the heat and immediately add the flour all at once, beating with a wooden spoon until the mixture forms a ball in the centre of the saucepan. Leave to cool for 3 minutes.

3 Add the eggs a little at a time, beating well after each addition until the paste is smooth, shiny and of a piping consistency.

4 Spoon the mixture into a piping bag fitted with a plain nozzle. Sprinkle the oiled baking sheet with water. Pipe the mixture onto the baking sheet in 7.5 cm/3 inch lengths.

5 Bake in the preheated oven for 18–20 minutes, or until well risen and golden. Make a slit along the side of each eclair.

6 Return the eclairs to the oven for a further 2 minutes to dry out. Transfer to a wire rack and leave to cool.

7 Halve the passion fruit and scoop the pulp of 4 of the fruits into a bowl. Add the cream, kirsch and icing sugar and whip until the cream holds it shape. Carefully spoon or pipe into the eclairs.

8 Melt the chocolate in a small heatproof bowl set over a saucepan of simmering water and stir until smooth.

9 Leave the chocolate to cool slightly, then spread over the top of the eclairs. Scoop the seeds and pulp out of the remaining passion fruit. Sieve. Use the juice to drizzle around the eclairs when serving.

2

5

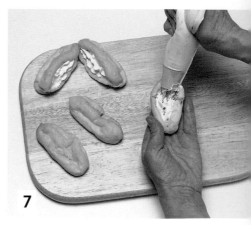

7

Chocolate Roulade

INGREDIENTS

Serves 8

150 g/5 oz golden caster sugar
5 medium eggs, separated
50 g/2 oz cocoa powder

For the filling:

300 ml/½ pint double cream
3 tbsp whisky
50 g/2 oz creamed coconut, chilled
2 tbsp icing sugar
coarsely shredded coconut, toasted

1 Preheat the oven to 180°C/350°F/Gas Mark 4, 10 minutes before baking. Oil and line a 33 x 23 cm /13 x 9 inch Swiss roll tin with a single sheet of non-stick baking parchment. Dust a large sheet of baking parchment with 2 tablespoons of the caster sugar.

2 Place the egg yolks in a bowl with the remaining sugar, set over a saucepan of gently simmering water and whisk until pale and thick. Sift the cocoa powder into the mixture and carefully fold in.

3 Whisk the egg whites in a clean, grease-free bowl until soft peaks form. Gently add 1 tablespoon of the whisked egg whites into the chocolate mixture then fold in the remaining whites. Spoon the mixture onto the prepared tin, smoothing the mixture into the corners. Bake in the preheated oven for 20–25 minutes, or until risen and springy to the touch.

4 Turn the cooked roulade out onto the sugar-dusted baking parchment and carefully peel off the lining paper. Cover with a clean damp tea towel and leave to cool.

5 To make the filling, pour the cream and whisky into a bowl and whisk until the cream holds its shape. Grate in the chilled creamed coconut, add the icing sugar and gently stir in. Uncover the roulade and spoon about three-quarters of coconut cream on the roulade and roll up. Spoon the remaining cream on the top and sprinkle with the coconut, then serve.

HELPFUL HINT

Take care when rolling up the roulade in this recipe as it can break up quite easily.

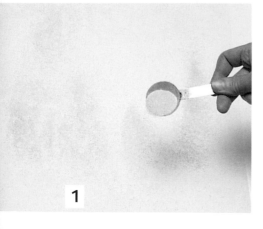

1

3

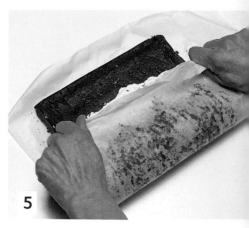

5

Chocolate Meringue Nest with Fruity Filling

INGREDIENTS

Serves 8

125 g/4 oz hazelnuts, toasted

125 g/4 oz golden caster sugar

75 g/3 oz plain dark chocolate, broken
  into pieces

2 medium egg whites

pinch of salt

1 tsp cornflour

½ tsp white wine vinegar

chocolate curls, to decorate

For the filling:

150 ml/¼ pint double cream

150 g/5 oz mascarpone cheese

prepared summer fruits, such
  as strawberries, raspberries
  and redcurrants

HELPFUL HINT

To make chocolate curls, melt the chocolate over hot water then pour onto a cool surface, preferably marble if available. Leave until just set but not hard, then using a large cook's knife or a cheese parer, push the blade at an angle across the surface of the chocolate to form curls.

1   Preheat the oven to 110°C/225°F/Gas Mark 1, 5 minutes before baking and line a baking sheet with non-stick baking parchment. Place the hazelnuts and 2 tablespoons of the caster sugar in a food processor and blend to a powder. Add the chocolate and blend again until the chocolate is roughly chopped.

2   In a clean, grease-free bowl, whisk the egg whites and salt until soft peaks form. Gradually whisk in the remaining sugar a teaspoonful at a time and continue to whisk until the meringue is stiff and shiny. Fold in the cornflour and the white wine vinegar with the chocolate and hazelnut mixture.

3   Spoon the mixture into 8 mounds, about 10 cm/4 inches in diameter, on the baking parchment. Do not worry if not perfect shapes. Make a hollow in each mound, then place in the preheated oven. Cook for 1½ hours, then switch the oven off and leave in the oven until cool.

4   To make the filling, whip the cream until soft peaks form. In another bowl, beat the mascarpone cheese until it is softened, then mix with the cream. Spoon the mixture into the meringue nests and top with the fresh fruits. Decorate with a few chocolate curls and serve.

1

2

3

Crème Brûlée with Sugared Raspberries

INGREDIENTS

Serves 6

600 ml/1 pint fresh whipping cream
4 medium egg yolks
75 g/3 oz caster sugar
½ tsp vanilla essence
25 g/1 oz demerara sugar
175 g/6 oz fresh raspberries

HELPFUL HINT

Most chefs use blow torches to brown the sugar in step 7, as this is the quickest way to caramelise the top of the dessert. Take great care if using a blow torch, especially when lighting. Otherwise use the grill, making sure that it is very hot and the dessert is thoroughly chilled before caramelising the sugar topping. This will prevent the custard underneath from melting.

1 Preheat the oven to 150°C/300°F/Gas Mark 2. Pour the cream into a bowl and place over a saucepan of gently simmering water. Heat gently but do not allow to boil.

2 Meanwhile, whisk together the egg yolks, 50 g/2 oz of the caster sugar and the vanilla essence. When the cream is warm, pour it over the egg mixture briskly whisking until it is mixed completely.

3 Pour into 6 individual ramekin dishes and place in a roasting tin.

4 Fill the tin with sufficient water to come halfway up the sides of the dishes.

5 Bake in the preheated oven for about 1 hour, or until the puddings are set. (To test if set, carefully insert a round bladed knife into the centre, if the knife comes out clean they are set.)

6 Remove the puddings from the roasting tin and allow to cool. Chill in the refrigerator, preferably overnight.

7 Sprinkle the sugar over the top of each dish and place the puddings under a preheated hot grill.

8 When the sugar has caramelised and turned deep brown, remove from the heat and cool. Chill the puddings in the refrigerator for 2–3 hours before serving.

9 Toss the raspberries in the remaining caster sugar and sprinkle over the top of each dish. Serve with a little extra cream if liked.

2

5

7

Chocolate, Orange & Pine Nut Tart

INGREDIENTS

Cuts into 8–10 slices

For the sweet shortcrust pastry:
150 g/5 oz plain flour
½ tsp salt
3–4 tbsp icing sugar
125 g/4 oz unsalted butter, diced
2 medium egg yolks, beaten
½ tsp vanilla essence

For the filling:
125 g/4 oz plain dark
  chocolate, chopped
60 g/2½ oz pine nuts,
  lightly toasted
2 large eggs
grated zest of 1 orange
1 tbsp Cointreau
225 ml/8 fl oz whipping cream
2 tbsp orange marmalade

FOOD FACT
Cointreau is an orange-flavoured liqueur and is used in many recipes. You could substitute Grand Marnier or any other orange liqueur, if you prefer.

1 Preheat the oven to 200°C/400°F/Gas Mark 6, 15 minutes before baking. Place the flour, salt and sugar in a food processor with the butter and blend briefly. Add the egg yolks, 2 tablespoons of iced water and the vanilla essence and blend until a soft dough is formed. Remove and knead until smooth, wrap in clingfilm and chill in the refrigerator for 1 hour.

2 Lightly oil a 23 cm/9 inch loose-based flan tin. Roll the dough out on a lightly floured surface to a 28 cm/11 inch round and use to line the tin. Press into the sides of the flan tin, crimp the edges, prick the base with a fork and chill in the refrigerator for 1 hour. Bake blind in the preheated oven for 10 minutes. Remove and place on a baking sheet. Reduce the oven temperature to 190°C/375°F/Gas Mark 5.

3 To make the filling, sprinkle the chocolate and the pine nuts evenly over the base of the pastry case. Beat the eggs, orange zest, Cointreau and cream in a bowl until well blended, then pour over the chocolate and pine nuts.

4 Bake in the oven for 30 minutes, or until the pastry is golden and the custard mixture is just set. Transfer to a wire rack to cool slightly. Heat the marmalade with 1 tablespoon of water and brush over the tart. Serve warm or at room temperature.

1

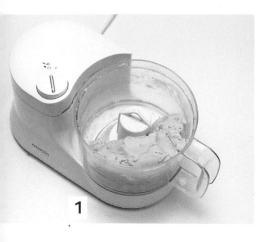

2

3

Pear & Chocolate Custard Tart

INGREDIENTS

Cuts into 6–8 slices

For the chocolate pastry:

125 g/4 oz unsalted butter, softened
60 g/2½ oz caster sugar
2 tsp vanilla essence
175 g/6 oz plain flour, sifted
40 g/1½ oz cocoa powder
whipped cream, to serve

For the filling:

125 g/4 oz plain dark
  chocolate, chopped
225 ml/8 fl oz whipping cream
50 g/2 oz caster sugar
1 large egg
1 large egg yolk
1 tbsp crème de cacao
3 ripe pears

HELPFUL HINT

The chocolate pastry is very soft so rolling it between sheets of clingfilm will make it much easier to handle without having to add a lot of extra flour.

1 Preheat the oven to 190°C/375°F/Gas Mark 5, 10 minutes before baking. To make the pastry, put the butter, sugar and vanilla essence into a food processor and blend until creamy. Add the flour and cocoa powder and process until a soft dough forms. Remove the dough, wrap in clingfilm and chill in the refrigerator for at least 1 hour.

2 Roll out the dough between 2 sheets of clingfilm to a 28 cm/11 inch round. Peel off the top sheet of clingfilm and invert the pastry round into a lightly oiled 23 cm/9 inch loose-based flan tin, easing the dough into the base and sides. Prick the base with a fork, then chill in the refrigerator for 1 hour.

3 Place a sheet of non-stick baking parchment and baking beans in the case and bake blind in the preheated oven for 10 minutes. Remove the parchment and beans and bake for a further 5 minutes. Remove and cool.

4 To make the filling, heat the chocolate, cream and half the sugar in a medium saucepan over a low heat, stirring until melted and smooth. Remove from the heat and cool slightly before beating in the egg, egg yolk and crème de cacao. Spread evenly over the pastry case base.

5 Peel the pears, then cut each pear in half and carefully remove the core. Cut each half crossways into thin slices and arrange over the custard, gently fanning the slices towards the centre and pressing into the chocolate custard. Bake in the oven for 10 minutes.

6 Reduce the oven temperature to 180°C/350°F/Gas Mark 4 and sprinkle the surface evenly with the remaining sugar. Bake in the oven for 20–25 minutes,or until the custard is set and the pears are tender and glazed. Remove from the oven and leave to cool slightly. Cut into slices, then serve with spoonfuls of whipped cream.

1

2

5

Double Chocolate Truffle Slice

INGREDIENTS

Cuts into 12–14 slices

1 quantity Chocolate Pastry
   (see page 232)
300 ml/½ pint double cream
300 g/11 oz plain dark
   chocolate, chopped
25–40 g/1–1½ oz unsalted
   butter, diced
50 ml/2 fl oz brandy or liqueur
icing sugar or cocoa powder
   for dusting

1 Preheat the oven to 200°C/400°F/Gas Mark 6, 15 minutes before baking. Prepare the chocolate pastry and chill in the refrigerator, according to instructions.

2 Roll the dough out to a rectangle about 38 x 15 cm/15 x 6 inches and use to line a rectangular loose-based flan tin, trim then chill in the refrigerator for 1 hour.

3 Place a sheet of non-stick baking parchment and baking beans in the pastry case, then bake blind in the preheated oven for 20 minutes. Remove the baking parchment and beans and bake for 10 minutes more. Leave to cool completely.

4 Bring the cream to the boil. Remove from the heat and add the chocolate all at once, stirring until melted and smooth. Beat in the butter, then stir in the brandy liqueur. Leave to cool slightly, then pour into the cooked pastry shell. Refrigerate until set.

5 Cut out 2.5 cm/1 inch strips of non-stick baking parchment. Place over the tart in a criss-cross pattern and dust with icing sugar or cocoa.

6 Arrange chocolate leaves, caraque or curls around the edges of the tart. Refrigerate until ready to serve. Leave to soften at room temperature for 15 minutes before serving.

TASTY TIP

Liqueurs that would work very well in this recipe include Tia Maria, Kahlua, Cointreau, Grand Marnier, Amaretto and Crème de Menthe.

3

4

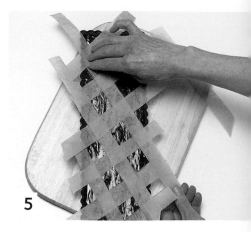

5

Mini Pistachio & Chocolate Strudels

INGREDIENTS
Makes 24

5 large sheets filo pastry
50 g/2 oz butter, melted
1–2 tbsp caster sugar for sprinkling
50 g/2 oz white chocolate, melted,
   to decorate

For the filling:
125 g/4 oz unsalted pistachios,
   finely chopped
3 tbsp caster sugar
50 g/2 oz plain dark chocolate,
   finely chopped
1–2 tsp rosewater
1 tbsp icing sugar for dusting

1 Preheat the oven to 170°C/325°F/Gas Mark 3, 10 minutes before baking. Lightly oil 2 large baking sheets. For the filling, mix the finely chopped pistachio nuts, the sugar and dark chocolate in a bowl. Sprinkle with the rosewater and stir lightly together and reserve.

2 Cut each filo pastry sheet into 4 to make 23 x 18 cm/ 9 x 7 inch rectangles. Place 1 rectangle on the work surface and brush with a little melted butter. Place another rectangle on top and brush with a little more butter. Sprinkle with a little caster sugar and spread about 1 dessertspoon of the filling along one short end. Fold the short end over the filling, then fold in the long edges and roll up. Place on the baking sheet seam-side down. Continue with the remaining pastry sheets and filling until both are used.

3 Brush each strudel with the remaining melted butter and sprinkle with a little caster sugar. Bake in the preheated oven for 20 minutes, or until golden brown and the pastry is crisp.

4 Remove from the oven and leave on the baking sheet for 2 minutes, then transfer to a wire rack. Dust with icing sugar. Place the melted white chocolate in a small piping bag fitted with a plain writing pipe and pipe squiggles over the strudel. Leave to set before serving.

TASTY TIP
Keep the unused filo pastry covered with a clean damp tea towel to prevent it from drying out.

1

2

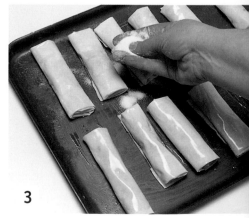

3

White Chocolate & Macadamia Tartlets

INGREDIENTS

Makes 10

1 quantity Sweet Shortcrust Pastry
(see page 230)
2 medium eggs
50 g/2 oz caster sugar
250 ml/9 fl oz golden syrup
40 g/1½ oz butter, melted
50 ml/2 fl oz whipping cream
1 tsp vanilla or almond essence
225 g/8 oz unsalted macadamia nuts,
coarsely chopped
150 g/5 oz white chocolate,
coarsely chopped

1 Preheat the oven to 200°C/400°F/Gas Mark 6, 15 minutes before baking. Roll the pastry out on a lightly floured surface and use to line 10 x 7.5–9 cm/3–3½ inch tartlet tins. Line each tin with a small piece of tinfoil and fill with baking beans. Arrange on a baking sheet and bake blind in the preheated oven for 10 minutes. Remove the tinfoil and baking beans and leave to cool.

2 Beat the eggs with the sugar until light and creamy, then beat in the golden syrup, the butter, cream and vanilla or almond essence. Stir in the macadamia nuts. Sprinkle 100 g/3½ oz of the chopped white chocolate equally over the bases of the tartlet cases and divide the mixture evenly among them.

3 Reduce the oven temperature to 180°C/350°F/Gas Mark 4 and bake the tartlets for 20 minutes, or until the tops are puffy and golden and the filling is set. Remove from the oven and leave to cool on a wire rack.

4 Carefully remove the tartlets from their tins and arrange closely together on the wire rack. Melt the remaining white chocolate and, using a teaspoon or a small paper piping bag, drizzle the melted chocolate over the surface of the tartlets in a zig-zag pattern. Serve slightly warm or at room temperature.

FOOD FACT

Macadamia nuts come from Hawaii and are large, crisp, buttery flavoured nuts. They are readily available from supermarkets.

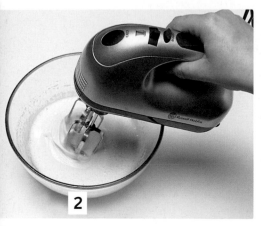
2

2

4

Chocolate Lemon Tartlets

INGREDIENTS

Makes 10

1 quantity Chocolate Pastry
  (see page 232)
175 ml/6 fl oz double cream
175 g/6 oz plain dark
  chocolate, chopped
2 tbsp butter, diced
1 tsp vanilla essence
350 g/12 oz lemon curd
225 ml/8 fl oz prepared custard sauce
225 ml/8 fl oz single cream
$\frac{1}{2}$ –1 tsp almond essence

To decorate:
grated chocolate
toasted flaked almonds

TASTY TIP

Lemon curd is very easy to make. In a medium-sized heatproof bowl, mix together 175 g/6 oz of caster sugar, the grated rind and juice of 2 large lemons and 4 large eggs. Add 125 g/4 oz cubed unsalted butter and place the bowl over a saucepan of gently simmering water. Stir often until thickened, about 20 minutes. Leave to cool and use as above.

1. Preheat the oven to 200°C/400°F/Gas Mark 6, 15 minutes before baking. Roll the prepared pastry out on a lightly floured surface and use to line 10 x 7.5 cm/3 inch tartlet tins. Place a small piece of crumpled tinfoil in each and bake blind in the preheated oven for 12 minutes. Remove from the oven and leave to cool.

2. Bring the cream to the boil, then remove from the heat and add the chocolate all at once. Stir until smooth and melted. Beat in the butter and vanilla essence and pour into the tartlets and leave to cool.

3. Beat the lemon curd until soft and spoon a thick layer over the chocolate in each tartlet, spreading gently to the edges. Do not chill in the refrigerator or the chocolate will be too firm.

4. Place the prepared custard sauce into a large bowl and gradually whisk in the cream and almond essence until the custard is smooth and runny.

5. To serve, spoon a little custard onto a plate and place a tartlet in the centre. Sprinkle with grated chocolate and almonds, then serve.

1

2

3

Raspberry Chocolate Ganache & Berry Tartlets

INGREDIENTS

Makes 10

1 quantity Chocolate Pastry
600 ml/1 pint whipping cream
275 g/10 oz seedless raspberry jam
225 g/8 oz plain dark chocolate, chopped
700 g/1½ lb raspberries or other summer berries
50 ml/2 fl oz framboise liqueur
1 tbsp caster sugar
crème fraîche, to serve

1 Preheat the oven to 200°C/400°F/Gas Mark 6, 15 minutes before cooking. Make the chocolate pastry and use to line 8 x 7.5 cm/3 inch tartlet tins. Bake blind in the preheated oven for 12 minutes.

2 Place 400 ml/14 fl oz of the cream and half of the raspberry jam in a saucepan and bring to the boil, whisking constantly to dissolve the jam. Remove from the heat and add the chocolate all at once, stirring until the chocolate has melted.

3 Pour into the pastry-lined tartlet tins, shaking gently to distribute the ganache evenly. Chill in the refrigerator for 1 hour or until set.

4 Place the berries in a large shallow bowl. Heat the remaining raspberry jam with half the framboise liqueur over a medium heat until melted and bubbling. Drizzle over the berries and toss gently to coat.

5 Divide the berries among the tartlets, piling them up if necessary. Chill in the refrigerator until ready to serve.

6 Remove the tartlets from the refrigerator for at least 30 minutes before serving. Using an electric whisk, whisk the remaining cream with the caster sugar and the remaining framboise liqueur until it is thick and softly peaking. Serve with the tartlets and crème fraîche.

1

2

3

Chocolate Raspberry Mille Feuille

INGREDIENTS

Serves 6

450 g/1 lb puff pastry, thawed
  if frozen
1 quantity Chocolate Raspberry
  Ganache (see page 244), chilled
700 g/1½ lbs fresh raspberries, plus
  extra for decorating
icing sugar for dusting

For the raspberry sauce:

225 g/8 oz fresh raspberries
2 tbsp seedless raspberry jam
1–2 tbsp caster sugar, or to taste
2 tbsp lemon juice or
  framboise liqueur

HELPFUL HINT

If you prefer, make 1 big mille feuille by leaving the 3 strips whole in step 2. Slice the finished mille feuille with a sharp serrated knife.

1 Preheat the oven to 200°C/400°F/Gas Mark 6, 15 minutes before baking. Lightly oil a large baking sheet and sprinkle with a little water. Roll out the pastry on a lightly floured surface to a rectangle about 43 x 28 cm/17 x 11 inches. Cut into 3 long strips. Mark each strip crossways at 6.5 cm/2½ inch intervals using a sharp knife; this will make cutting the baked pastry easier and neater. Carefully transfer to the baking sheet, keeping the edges as straight as possible.

2 Bake in the preheated oven for 20 minutes or until well risen and golden brown. Place on a wire rack and leave to cool. Carefully transfer each rectangle to a work surface and, using a sharp knife, trim the long edges straight. Cut along the knife marks to make 18 rectangles.

3 Place all the ingredients for the raspberry sauce in a food processor and blend until smooth. If the purée is too thick, add a little water. Taste and adjust the sweetness if necessary. Strain into a bowl, cover and chill in the refrigerator.

4 Place 1 pastry rectangle on the work surface flat-side down, spread with a little chocolate ganache and sprinkle with a few fresh raspberries. Spread a second rectangle with a little ganache, place over the first, pressing gently, then sprinkle with a few raspberries. Place a third rectangle on top, flat-side up, and spread with a little chocolate ganache.

5 Arrange some raspberries on top and dust lightly with a little icing sugar. Repeat with the remaining pastry rectangles, chocolate ganache and fresh raspberries.

6 Chill in the refrigerator until required and serve with the raspberry sauce and any remaining fresh raspberries.

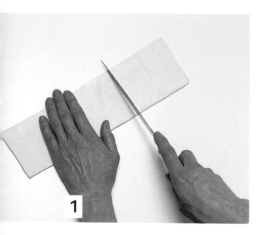

1

2

5

Sachertorte

INGREDIENTS

Cuts into 10–12 slices

150 g/5 oz plain dark chocolate
150 g/5 oz unsalted butter, softened
125 g/4 oz caster sugar, plus
  2 tbsp
3 medium eggs, separated
150 g/5 oz plain flour, sifted

To decorate:

225 g/8 oz apricot jam
125 g/4 oz plain dark
  chocolate, chopped
125 g/4 oz unsalted butter
25 g/1 oz milk chocolate

FOOD FACT

In 1832, the Viennese foreign minister asked a Vienna hotel to prepare an especially tempting cake. The head pastry chef was ill and so the task fell to second-year apprentice, Franz Sacher, who presented this delightful cake.

1 Preheat the oven to 180°C/350°F/Gas Mark 4, 10 minutes before baking. Lightly oil and line a deep 23 cm/9 inch cake tin.

2 Melt the 150 g/5 oz of chocolate in a heatproof bowl set over a pan of simmering water. Stir in 1 tablespoon of water and leave to cool.

3 Beat the butter and 125 g/4 oz of the sugar together until light and fluffy. Beat in the egg yolks, one at a time, beating well between each addition. Stir in the melted chocolate, then the flour.

4 In a clean grease-free bowl, whisk the egg whites until stiff peaks form, then whisk in the remaining sugar. Fold into the chocolate mixture and spoon into the prepared tin. Bake in the pre-heated oven for 30 minutes until firm. Leave for 5 minutes, then turn out onto a wire rack to cool. Leave the cake upside down.

5 To decorate the cake, split the cold cake in 2 and place one half on a serving plate. Heat the jam and rub through a fine sieve.

6 Spread half the jam onto the first cake half, then cover with the remaining cake layer and spread over the remaining jam. Leave at room temperature for 1 hour or until the jam has set.

7 Place the plain dark chocolate with the butter into a heatproof bowl set over a saucepan of simmering water and heat until the chocolate has melted. Stir until smooth, then leave until thickened. Use to cover the cake.

8 Melt the milk chocolate in a heatproof bowl set over a saucepan of simmering water. Place in a small greaseproof piping bag and snip a small hole at the tip. Pipe Sacher with a large 'S' on the top. Leave to set at room temperature.

3

4

5

White Chocolate & Raspberry Mousse Gateau

INGREDIENTS

Cuts 8 slices

4 medium eggs
125 g/4 oz caster sugar
75 g/3 oz plain flour, sifted
25 g/1 oz cornflour, sifted
3 gelatine leaves
450 g/1 lb raspberries, thawed
   if frozen
400 g/14 oz white chocolate
200 g/7 oz plain fromage frais
2 medium egg whites
25 g/1 oz caster sugar
4 tbsp raspberry or orange liqueur
200 ml/7 fl oz double cream
fresh raspberries, halved, to decorate

HELPFUL HINT

Do not try to wrap the chocolate-covered parchment around the cake before it is nearly set or it will run down and be uneven.

1 Preheat the oven to 190°C/375°F/Gas Mark 5, 10 minutes before baking. Oil and line 2 x 23 cm/9 inch cake tins. Whisk the eggs and sugar until thick and creamy and the whisk leaves a trail in the mixture. Fold in the flour and cornflour, then divide between the tins. Bake in the preheated oven for 12–15 minutes or until risen and firm. Cool in the tins, then turn out onto wire racks.

2 Place the gelatine with 4 tablespoons of cold water in a dish and leave to soften for 5 minutes. Purée half the raspberries, press through a sieve, then heat until nearly boiling. Squeeze out excess water from the gelatine, add to the purée and stir until dissolved. Reserve.

3 Melt 175 g/6 oz of the chocolate in a bowl set over a saucepan of simmering water. Leave to cool, then stir in the fromage frais and purée. Whisk the egg whites until stiff and whisk in the sugar. Fold into the raspberry mixture with the rest of the raspberries.

4 Line the sides of a 23 cm/9 inch springform tin with non-stick baking parchment. Place 1 layer of sponge in the base and sprinkle with half the liqueur. Pour in the raspberry mixture and top with the second sponge. Brush with the remaining liqueur. Press down and chill in the refrigerator for 4 hours. Unmould onto a plate.

5 Cut a strip of double thickness non-stick baking parchment to fit around the cake and stand 1 cm/½ inch higher. Melt the remaining white chocolate and spread thickly onto the parchment. Leave until just setting. Wrap around the cake and freeze for 15 minutes. Peel away the parchment. Whip the cream until thick and spread over the top. Decorate with raspberries.

1

2

4

French Chocolate Pecan Torte

INGREDIENTS

Cuts into 16 slices

200 g/7 oz plain dark
  chocolate, chopped
150 g/5 oz butter, diced
4 large eggs
100 g/3½ oz caster sugar
2 tsp vanilla essence
125 g/4 oz pecans, finely ground
2 tsp ground cinnamon
24 pecan halves, lightly toasted,
  to decorate

For the chocolate glaze:

125 g/4 oz plain dark
  chocolate, chopped
60 g/2½ oz butter, diced
2 tbsp clear honey
¼ tsp ground cinnamon

FOOD FACT

Although this recipe is French, the torte actually originates from Germany, and tends to be a very rich cake-like dessert. It is delicious served with a fruity mixed berry compote.

1 Preheat the oven to 180°C/350°F/Gas Mark 4, 10 minutes before baking. Lightly butter and line a 20.5 x 5 cm/8 x 2 inch springform tin with non-stick baking paper. Wrap the tin in a large sheet of tinfoil to prevent water seeping in.

2 Melt the chocolate and butter in a saucepan over a low heat and stir until smooth. Remove from the heat and cool.

3 Using an electric whisk, beat the eggs, sugar and vanilla essence until light and foamy. Gradually beat in the melted chocolate, ground nuts and cinnamon, then pour into the prepared tin.

4 Set the foil-wrapped tin in a large roasting tin and pour in enough boiling water to come 2 cm/¾ inches up the sides of the tin. Bake in the preheated oven until the edge is set, but the centre is still soft when the tin is gently shaken. Remove from the oven and place on a wire rack to cool.

5 For the glaze, melt all the ingredients over a low heat until melted and smooth, then remove from the heat. Dip each pecan halfway into the glaze and set on a sheet of non-stick baking paper until set. Allow the remaining glaze to thicken slightly.

6 Remove the cake from the tin and invert. Pour the glaze over the cake smoothing the top and spreading the glaze around the sides. Arrange the glazed pecans around the edge of the torte. Allow to set and serve.

Chocolate & Almond Daquoise with Summer Berries

INGREDIENTS

Serves 8

For the almond meringues:

6 large egg whites

¼ tsp cream of tartar

275 g/10 oz caster sugar

½ tsp almond essence

50 g/2 oz blanched or flaked almonds, lightly toasted and finely ground

For the chocolate buttercream:

75 g/3 oz butter, softened

450 g/1 lb icing sugar, sifted

50 g/2 oz cocoa powder, sifted

3–4 tbsp milk or single cream

550 g/1¼ lb mixed summer berries such as raspberries, strawberries and blackberries

To decorate:

toasted flaked almonds

icing sugar

1 Preheat the oven to 140°C/ 275°F/Gas Mark 1 10 minutes before baking. Line 3 baking sheets with non-stick baking paper and draw a 20.5 cm/8 inch round on each one.

2 Whisk the egg whites and cream of tartar until soft peaks form. Gradually beat in the sugar, 2 tablespoons at a time, beating well after each addition, until the whites are stiff and glossy.

3 Beat in the almond essence, then using a metal spoon or rubber spatula gently fold in the ground almonds.

4 Divide the mixture evenly between the 3 circles of baking paper, spreading neatly into the rounds and smoothing the tops evenly.

5 Bake in the preheated oven for about 11/4 hours or until crisp, rotating the baking sheets halfway through cooking. Turn off the oven, allow to cool for about 1 hour, then remove and cool completely before discarding the lining paper

6 Beat the butter, icing sugar and cocoa powder until smooth and creamy, adding the milk or cream to form a soft consistency.

7 Reserve about a quarter of the berries to decorate. Spread 1 meringue with a third of the buttercream and top with a third of the remaining berries. Repeat with the other meringue rounds, buttercream and berries.

8 Scatter with the toasted flaked almonds, the reserved berries and sprinkle with icing sugar and serve.

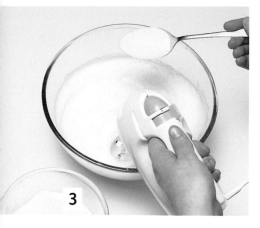

3

6

7

Index